S0-AAE-967

EVERYTHING YOU WANT
TO KNOW ABOUT

FORTUNE
TELLING
WITH CARDS

Karma System

Gypsy System

Professional System

Palmistry

by ZOLAR

ARCO PUBLISHING COMPANY, INC.

New York

Published by Arco Publishing Company, Inc.
219 Park Avenue South, New York, N.Y. 10003

Library of Congress Catalog Card Number 72-3138
ISBN 0-668-02659-6

Printed in the United States of America

All letters and communications to ZOLAR
should be addressed to:

ZOLAR
333 West 52nd Street
New York, N.Y. 10019

FORTUNE TELLING
WITH CARDS

From time immemorial there has been a universal curiosity as to what the future has in store. It is human nature to want to know what tomorrow and the future in general may bring.

Beyond the portals of today Destiny holds the secret of love, health, wealth, travel, marriage; happiness with sweethearts, husbands or wives; success, fame, fortune, inheritances, etc. From antiquity a deck of playing cards has seemed to hold the answers to these interesting questions of life.

A deck of ordinary playing cards has come to mean a great many things. . . . The almost endless mathematical combinations that are possible with a deck of cards is nothing short of a mystery. Among certain people in the past a deck of cards was considered the "instrument of the devil," because in the frontier days, before there were many books and newspapers, or other diversions men amused themselves with various games played with cards. Since some ill-tempered men became angry when they lost, each man carried a gun to protect himself. In those days a man also carried a gun to protect himself from wild beasts, or from the attacks of Indians. Naturally, an angry man in an argument would reach for his gun if he was carrying one. However, gambling did not originate with playing cards. Men used to gamble on many events; on the weather, for example, or the successful outcome of a venture. Some men in the distant past, no doubt, thought of the possibility of gambling with playing cards. That is how the idea of gambling became connected in the minds of many people with playing cards.

Playing cards are no more evil than some other practices in vogue today. One may read evil into anything. Let us look farther back into history and learn some interesting things about a deck of cards.

Various forms of playing cards closely resembling those of today, it has been discovered, were used by the ancient Celtic races. The Gypsies of central Russia devised a set of playing cards that were later used in clairvoyance and in divining the future. The fame of their predictions spread to Greece and the Roman Empire. A set of simple "cards" fashioned in stone were used by the ancient Egyptians. The Chaldeans used a series of "cards" molded from clay to designate certain things that they saw in the stars. Discoveries show that many generations of ancients used some form of playing cards for amusement or divination.

It remained for some of the early Christians to give the cards a special meaning or reason for being. Formerly there was only one suit to a deck of cards. Their representations were as follows:

Ace represents One or All; One God, One Universe.

Two Spot represents God (Father) and Son.

Three Spot represents God (Father), Son, and Holy Ghost.

Four Spot represents the Four "corners" of the Earth.

Five Spot represents God in the midst of the World.

Six Spot represents the number of days it took for Creation.

Seven Spot represents mystery or the day of rest.

Eight Spot represents the seven planets and the Moon.

Nine Spot represents the major constellations in the sky.

Ten Spot represents the completed Universe of 10 planets and satellites.

And then in honor of the nation the "Royal House" was represented by:

The Jack: the court servant.

The Queen: the female ruler of the nation.

The King: the male ruler of the nation.

As time marched on, the various Suits were added to the deck of cards, each of which corresponded to certain ideals dear to the hearts of the inventors.

The modern deck of playing cards contains Four Suits corresponding to the four seasons of the year. Twelve face cards represent the twelve journeys of the Sun or months of the year. There are 52 cards in a deck denoting the number of weeks in the year, and 365 spots representing the number of days in the year.

There are many other symbolical mysteries in a deck of cards that space does not permit me to indicate here. Suffice it to know that the deck of cards was scientifically conceived and the only evil that can be connected with them is the use man in his ignorance puts them to.

For many generations past, it has been a well-known fact that a person who could tell fortunes by any method has had a good deal of popularity and entertainment from this ability. Various systems of fortune telling have come down to us from the past, many of them long since forgotten, but the pleasure of card reading has survived. Even today there are thousands of people who are strongly interested in this diversion, either because they actually believe in such predictions, as the ancients did, or because they are interested in it only as entertainment. At any rate it is always of interest to have your fortune told.

THE KARMA SYSTEM

USING 32 CARDS

This system of Card Reading is known as the Karma System of Fortune Telling with Ordinary Playing Cards, and is perhaps the simplest system known.

On a large sheet of paper or cardboard you first draw 12 squares and number them as follows:

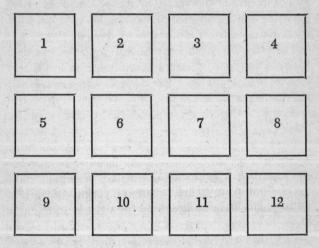

The Number in these squares represents days or weeks or months. Fortunes told with this system are supposed to happen within 12 months. If a person wants the numbers to represent weeks he should state this at the beginning of the layout, likewise, if the person wishes it to represent days or months collectively.

As you gain practice with this system you will automatically memorize these spaces and numbers so that you will not need the chart of squares before you.

You now take a deck of ordinary cards and remove all of the 2, 3, 4, 5, and 6-spots and lay them to one side. You will now have left in your deck the Aces, Kings, Queens, Jacks, tens, nines, eights, and sevens.

Hand the deck of cards to your client and ask him or her to shuffle the cards thoroughly and at the same time to make a silent wish. If you are telling your own fortune shuffle them yourself and make a silent wish. For simplicity we will suppose that you are telling your own fortune. After thoroughly shuffling and wishing, cut the cards in three piles. Place them so that the motion of cutting the cards will be towards you. Now turn up the three piles and count the spots on the upturned cards. Jacks count 20; Queens count 25 and Kings count 30. The total of these three cards will be your "lucky number" for the day, the week or the month, as the case may be. If the 9 of hearts turns up, you will get your wish immediately. If you do not cut the card, you will find out later when you will get your wish, if at all.

You will now put the three piles back together and shuffle them until your "hunch" tells you to stop. Next, remember that a 7-spot is an indicator card and must never be put in any of the squares on your chart. When you have finished shuffling hold the deck in your right hand, backs up. Start dealing them off one at a time, laying them on the table before you face up. Continue to deal them off one at a time until a 7-spot turns up. This is your indicator card. Now take the very next card and lay it face up in Square number 1 on your chart. Proceed until you come to another 7-spot and lay the card following that in Square number 2 on your chart. When you have gone through the deck, pick it up and shuffle it again until your "hunch" tells you to stop and go through the same process with the 7-spots again. Continue this process until all of the Squares on your Chart are filled with cards.

NOTE:—When two 7-spots turn up together that operation is "killed" and you replace the two 7-spots in the deck (not together) and proceed to the next 7-spot. Do not use the card following a double 7. Ordinarily you will go through the deck 3 times to fill all the spaces in your chart—but if you have several double 7's you may have to go through the deck several times before you have all the squares filled. A double 7 shows that you did not shuffle them enough—or the cards are not placed right for your particular fortune. You will not be able to get them out of the deck until they are properly placed according to your destiny, following the single 7's until all the spaces are filled in your chart. Remember, do NOT place a 7-spot in any of the squares.

When all of the Squares are filled you are then ready for the second operation which is very simple indeed. Shuffle the deck until your conscience tells you to stop. Then deal off the cards one by one in the order that they come from the top of the deck and place one card over each of the cards already on your chart. You may lay them crosswise or corner-wise so that you can still see what card is underneath. Start in the upper left-hand corner at Square number 1 and cover each of the 12 cards in this manner with one card each. The cards that you have left in your hand now you may lay aside for you will not need them any more.

NOTE:—In this Second operation you may place the 7-spots on the chart if they show up, for you are finished with them as indicator cards, since you are dealing those top cards onto your Chart from the deck in the order that they are in. Remember in this second operation you forget about an "indicator card" and just deal them off from the top of the deck one by one. You are now ready to begin your translation. Refer to the list below.

Meaning of the Cards

The following table gives the literal meaning of the various cards in the Four Suits. You will combine meanings and balance them according to what cards appear together in any of the squares on your chart. By studying the example given on Page 4 you will soon learn how to read the cards after you have them laid out on your cardboard chart.

HEARTS

ACE

Always pertains to home affairs. The card over it or under it will denote the nature of the home affairs.

KING

Thoughts of, influence of, or association with an elderly or middle-aged man of medium light complexion. Possibly a bald-headed or partly gray-haired gentleman of medium complexion.

QUEEN

Thoughts of, influence of, or association with a medium light complexioned lady. Nature of the part played by the lady will be indicated by the other card in the same square with her.

JACK

Thoughts of, influence of, or association with a medium light complexioned young man. If a red card is in the same square with him it is favorable; if a black card it is unfavorable.

TEN

Always denotes a brilliant future. Hopes, ambitions and plans. If accompanied with a red card no interference. If accompanied with a black card some delays in realizing ambitions.

NINE

This is the "wish card." If it shows up anywhere, the wish made while shuffling the cards will come true, but will be controlled by the card appearing with it in the square. Also it will come true within the number of days, weeks or months indicated by the number square in which it appears. If in the 2nd square it will mature in two days, weeks or months.

EIGHT

Denotes love, affection, sympathy, consolation and favors from other people. It will be tempered or influenced by the card with it in the square.

SEVEN

Denotes a very pleasant surprise. If a face card appears with it in the square you may describe the person the favor comes from. If some other card appears with it, you will be surprised to hear of that particular piece of news, whatever the nature of the card is.

DIAMONDS

ACE

Always pertains to a letter or message that is to be received. The other card in the square with it denotes the nature of the letter or message. If a face card appears with it, the letter or message will come from a person fitting that description.

KING

Thoughts of, influence of, or association with a very light or possibly a gray-haired, middle-aged or elderly gentleman.

QUEEN

Thoughts of, influence of, or association with a light blonde lady. The card appearing with it denotes the nature of this association.

JACK

Thoughts of, influence of, or association with a very blond young man. If with a red card—good results. If with a black card—disappointing results.

TEN

Big money—large amounts of money are denoted by the Ten of Diamonds. Ease or difficulty in obtaining it will be shown by the accompanying card with it in the square. If a red card—ease—if a black card—difficulty.

NINE

Indicates inheritance, or receipt of extra money aside from the regular source of income. If a red card is with it the amount will be quite large; if a black card is with it the amount will be small or there may be some trouble over it. If a face card is with it the money comes through the influence of a person who fits the description of the card.

EIGHT

Receipt of money owing, or a gift of a small amount of money. If a face card is with it, the money comes from a person who fits the description of the card.

SEVEN

Receipt of a surprise present. If with a face card it means the renewal of an old friendship that will be pleasing.

CLUBS

ACE

Denotes a marriage or news of a marriage that is reasonably close. If it appears with a card that fits your description it may be you or some member of your family who will marry.

KING

Thoughts of, influence of, or association with a middle-aged, medium dark gentleman. The card appearing with it in the square denotes the way he will show up in your fortune.

QUEEN

Thoughts of, influence of, or association with a medium brunette lady. If with a red card it is favorable; if with a black card it is unfavorable.

JACK

Thoughts of, influence of, or association with a medium dark young man. Nature of the association is indicated by the card in the square with it.

TEN

Usually denotes business worry. If with a red card the worry will not last long. If with a black card the worry may continue for some time.

NINE

This card has no special meaning of its own. It only means "for sure." It intensifies the meaning of the card appearing in the square with it. If a face card is with it, the meaning is that you will meet that particular person for certain.

EIGHT

Anxiety. You feel uncertain and somewhat anxious about something, probably in business or working conditions.

SEVEN

Denotes a slight delay in some plans. The nature of

these plans will be revealed by the card appearing with it in the square.

SPADES

ACE

Signifies trouble, slander, gossip and intrigues. If a red card is in the square with it, it will not amount to much. If a black card is with it, it will annoy you for quite some time.

KING

Thoughts of, influence of, or association with a rather dark complexioned, middle-aged or elderly gentleman.

QUEEN

Thoughts of, influence of, or association with a brunette lady. If with a red card, results are favorable. If with a black card the results will be unsatisfactory.

JACK

Thoughts of, influence of or association with a very dark complexioned young man; likely brown eyes, black hair and ruddy skin. The nature of the association will be revealed by the card in the same square with it.

TEN

This card denotes news of death or very severe illness. If a red card is with it, the news will not affect you much and it will be someone distant in affections.

If a black card goes with it, the news comes from a relative or close friend.

NINE

Reverses in personal affairs or worries in business. If with a red card they will not be serious. If with a black card they will continue for a time.

EIGHT

Drastic actions, or threats. Nothing necessarily serious, mostly persistent annoyances to your peace of mind. If with a red card they will soon be over. If with a black card you will be annoyed for some time.

SEVEN

Disappointment in some plans. If with a red card they will eventually materialize even though delayed. If with a black card you might as well abandon the idea for the present and concentrate on something else.

After a little practice you will memorize what each card indicates and will not have to refer to the above lists.

Most people who are interested in fortune telling with cards are mediumistically inclined. While laying out the cards for a friend or any other person who wishes you to read the cards for them, if you feel impelled to add something more to what the cards mean, be sure to add these impressions to the fortune, for often to a psychically inclined person the cards act as a "concentration point," through which information of a valuable nature sometimes comes.

After you have looked up all the meanings of the

cards in the squares, take notice of the layout. If two face cards appear together in any square it means a brother and sister if they are both of the same suit; a wife and husband if opposite suits. Two Queens mean sisters or companions or partners. Two Jacks mean brothers, pals or partners. King and Jack means father and son or possibly partners.

You will now forget the squares entirely. You look at the layout. See if there are any cards on the bottom or top of the same number or denomination beside each other. The meanings are the same regardless of whether they are on the top or bottom, but alternately they do not count, such as an Ace on the bottom in one pile and an Ace on the top of it. They must both be together on the top or both on the bottom to count.

The meaning of cards that are the same denomination which are side of each other are as follows:

ACES side of each other: Change of place, which could either be residence or business. If two black ones the change in unfavorable. If a black and a red one the change is doubtful and must be given careful thought and consideration.

KINGS side of each other: You will be conversing or having some dealing with an officer of the law.

QUEENS side of each other: You will have a pleasant new friendship that will be very inspiring to you. If both Queens are black the friend will be dark. If red Queens, the friend will be medium complexioned.

JACKS side of each other: You will change your affections from one person to another. Denotes a change in close associations. If both Jacks are red, the change will be permanent. If black the change will be temporary. If alternate red and black the change will keep you in an uncertain attitude.

TENS side of each other: Change of times. By this is meant change in conditions and environment around you. If both are red the change will be most successful. If they are both black, the change will not prove satisfactory and you are advised to prevent it. If alternate in color the change will be satisfactory.

NINES side of each other: A change in business is about to take place. If they are both black it will be necessary for you to keep close watch on business conditions to prevent complications in the changes that are coming. If they are both red the change will be satisfactory but not necessarily beneficial.

EIGHTS side of each other: You are to take a trip into another state. If both are red the trip will prove to be both pleasant and profitable. If both are black the trip will be attended with delays, disappointments and uncertain conditions, so it would be best not to take the trip. If the colors alternate; that is if one is red and the other black the trip will be pleasant but not necessarily profitable.

SEVENS side of each other: A series of sudden developments, all of them of a minor nature, that will change some of your personal plans. These changes come as a surprise. If both are red the changes are for the best. If they are both black the changes will delay you somewhat and you are advised to be reluctant in entertaining such changes. If colors are alternate then the changes will cause about the same results as your original plans.

The next thing that you will look for in this layout is the number of face cards showing. If there are 6 or more face cards showing, you are going to be in a crowd of people very soon. It may be a party, dance, lecture, or something like that, where large crowds of people gather. If all of the Queens are showing the crowd will be equally divided as to males and females. If one or two Queens are missing then the crowd will be mostly of men. If all of the Queens are showing and one or more Kings are missing the crowd will be mostly women.

You will now count the number of Hearts showing in the layout. If there are 6 or more hearts showing you will have a goodly amount of love and affection throughout the coming days, weeks or months according to whatever time you have set for this Fortune to cover.

Next count the number of Diamonds. If there are 6 or more Diamonds showing you will handle a great deal of money during the time covered by the Fortune.

Now count the number of Clubs showing. If there are 6 or more Clubs showing you will be concentrating a great deal on business affairs during the time covered by the Fortune.

Lastly count the number of Spades showing. If there are 6 or more spades showing you will be much concerned about your domestic life during the time covered by the Fortune.

NOTE—When counting the number of cards in the Suits, include the Face cards in this checkup.

Example of a Fortune

We will now lay out the cards on the chart. Follow closely this sample fortune, so that you will become familiar with the translating of the cards. Get your deck of cards and lay them out as follows:

In Square Number 1 put the 8 of Diamonds. On top of it lay the Queen of Clubs.

In Square Number 2 put the 10 of Clubs. On top of it put the Ace of Diamonds.

In Square Number 3 put the 10 of Diamonds. On top of it put the King of Clubs.

In Square Number 4 put the Queen of Diamonds. On top of it put the King of Spades.

In Square Number 5 put the 10 of Hearts. On top of it put the Seven of Diamonds.

In Square Number 6 put the 8 of Hearts. On top of it put the Jack of Spades.

In Square Number 7 put the 9 of Spades. On top of it put the Jack of Hearts.

In Square Number 8 put the Ace of Clubs. On top of it put the Queen of Spades.

In Square Number 9 put the Jack of Diamonds. On top of it put the Ace of Spades.

In Square Number 10 put the 9 of Clubs. On top of it put the Queen of Hearts.

In Square Number 11 put the Ace of Hearts. On top of it put the Seven of Hearts.

In Square Number 12 put the 9 of Hearts. On top of it put the Nine of Diamonds.

We are supposing that you went through the deck with the ordinary proceedings and the layout on the chart now is the result. We are now ready to begin the translating of the cards. Start with Square Number 1. Begin the reading in this manner:

"There is a dark lady, probably a medium brunette, through whose influence you are to receive a small amount of money. The money may come from her or it may come through her influence; at any rate in receiving this amount of money you will have some association with this brunette lady. Since this is in Square Number 1, it will occur within 1 day, 1 week, or 1 month.

Now refer to Square Number 2. The Ace of Diamonds means that you are to receive within 2 days, weeks or months a letter containing a great deal of information about business worries that the writer is deeply concerned about. The letter probably comes from a close friend or relative; at any rate someone close enough that their business worry would concern you. Notice if on the bottom of each side of the 10 of Clubs there is a red card—this indicates that the person's business worries will not last long. (If there should be any black cards surrounding the 10 of Clubs on the bottom, the worries of the person in whom you are interested will not be overcome soon).

Now refer to Square Number 3. Through the influence of a medium-dark, elderly or middle-aged gentleman you are to receive a rather large sum of money. This is to come within 3 days, weeks or months.

Refer now to Square Number 4. There are two face cards in this square. Therefore we will say: within 4 days, weeks or months you are to have some pleasant association with a rather dark, middle-aged gentleman and his wife who is either gray or very light complexioned. Since the gentleman is middle-aged, the wife is probably gray. Therefore it is quite safe to say that you will have association with a dark elderly gentleman and his gray-haired wife. The nature of this association is not shown, however it is important enough to show up in your Fortune, so it will probably be a reasonably pleasant association since there is a red card beside the Queen on the bottom. (Remember that the more important cards are always the ones on the bottom.)

Next is Square Number 5. The 7 of Diamonds on top of the 10 of Hearts will be translated in this manner. Within 5 days, weeks or months you will be in receipt of a gift or assistance from someone which will agreeably affect your future. Denotes a very encouraging outlook for your future since there is a red card on every side of the 10 of Hearts on the bottom.

In Square Number 6 is the Jack of Spades on top of the 8 of Hearts. This denotes that you are to have close association with a dark-complexioned young man who is very much in love with someone and he will tell you all about it. If the person having their Fortune told happens to be a young unmarried lady in love with this dark, handsome young man then this square would mean something important is to happen within the 6 days, weeks or months, because it occurs in Square Number 6.

The Jack of Hearts is on top of the 9 of Spades in Square Number 7. A medium light young man of your acquaintance is going to have some reverses or troubles in his personal affairs and may come to you for consolation. You may tell him that his troubles are not as serious as they seem, because there is a majority of red cards surrounding the 9 of Spades on the bottom.

Square Number 8 shows that a very dark brunette lady of your acquaintance is going to get married within 8 days, weeks or months. On the top and bottom side of the Ace of Clubs (marriage) there is a red card; therefore the marriage will be quite satisfactory, but the black card to the left side of the Ace of Clubs indicates that there will be a few differences of opinion between them occasionally.

In Square Number 9, the Ace of Spades on top of the Jack of Diamonds denotes that a rather light-complexioned young male friend of yours is to get mixed up in some slander, gossip and confusion that will worry him

very much, and you will hear all about it. He should
not take this too seriously, for above him on the bottom
is a red card and beside him is the 9 of Clubs which
is not a bad card—(look it up in the list of Clubs).
Therefore he will get out of his troubles without too
much difficulty.

Square Number 10 in this layout does not indicate
anything of importance. We can merely say that within ten days, weeks or months you will have some pleasant association with a medium-light lady, which looks
beneficial since there are all red cards surrounding the
9 of Clubs. We can say that you will have this association for sure—since the 9 of Clubs is the "for sure" card.

Square Number 11 is interesting. The 7 of Hearts on
top of the Ace of Hearts indicates that a very pleasant
surprise of some sort is coming into your home. The
surprise may come from a stranger, or it may come from
some member of the family. It is impossible to say
where it comes from, but the important part is that it
comes directly to your door, or right into your home.
And this, of course, will occur within 11 days, weeks
or months since these cards happen to be in Square
Number 11.

Square Number 12 is very interesting. When you
shuffled the cards and made a wish at the beginning of
the Fortune, you must have wished something about
money or inheritance. This square indicates that you
are going to get your wish whatever it might have been
within a 12; that is 12 days, weeks or months. It also
indicates that about the same time that you get your
wish you will also receive a gift of money, an inheritance or extra money from some source different from
your regular income.

NOTE:—If the 9 of Hearts had not shown up in this
layout it would have meant that you are not to get your

wish very soon. But if the Wish Card (9 on Hearts) does show up you must not tell your wish to a living soul until it materializes.

There are some people who are not fair and they will lay out their cards to see what is to happen to them in terms of days, and wish for a million dollars. This of course is ridiculous, and the person having their Fortune told must be instructed not to wish for impossible things but for reasonable things that could happen to them if Fate sees fit. The cards will tell if they are to get that particular wish or not. If one isn't serious or reasonable he should not have his fortune told.

Now that we have finished with the squares we will see what cards are beside each other in this layout. We find that there are two Tens beside each other in the top row on the bottom. Therefore you are going to have a change of the conditions surrounding you. The cards are alternate colors, so the change will be satisfactory.

Those are the only two cards on the bottom that are beside each other with the same denomination. You notice there are two Nines (9 of Hearts and 9 of Spades) on the bottom that are "cornerwise" to each other, but this does not count as the cards must be next to each other either vertically or horizontally.

Now we refer to the layer of cards on top. We find two Kings together on the top row. This indicates that you will be having some dealings or conversation with a policeman, judge, attorney, Justice of the Peace or some other person connected with the law. It doesn't mean that there is any special trouble in store, but that you will have some dealings with them that will likely be important, but not serious. If all black cards were around these Kings on the top row, it would mean that likely you would have some dispute or quarrel which

might result in your consulting an officer of the law.
But in this layout there is a red Jack below one of the
Kings and a red Ace to the left of one of the Kings.
Therefore we can say that it will likely just be a friend-
ly conversation.

On the second row we find two Jacks next to each
other on the top layer. This denotes that you are going
to change your affections from someone you are now
very fond of to another person. Since the Jacks are alternate colors the change will be to your present best
friend. If both Jacks were red it would perhaps be to a
person of approximately the same complexion as your
present. If both Jacks were black it would mean the
same, but when the colors alternate then the change
will be to a person opposite in description to your present lover or friend.

The two Nines on top of each other in Square 12 do
not count. They MUST be either horizontal or vertical
to each other. We are finished with this checkup, since
there are no other cards on the chart next to another
of the same denomination.

We now count the number of hearts on both the top
and bottom layers. There are 7 hearts showing on the
chart. This means that your life will be blessed with a
reasonable amount of love and affection in the time that
the Fortune covers, either in days, weeks or months.

Now we count the diamonds. There are 7 diamonds
on the chart. This means that for the duration of the
Fortune you will handle a considerable amount of
money.

Now count the clubs. There are only 5 clubs; therefore your mind will not be taken up with business as
much as with other things of life for the duration of
your Fortune, either weeks, days or months.

Lastly count the Spades. There are only 5 spades so
you will not be giving any special time or thought to

your domestic affairs for the time covered by your Fortune. You will merely follow your regular domestic routine.

We will now count the face cards. There are 9 face cards on the chart. The 4 Queens are there, but 2 Kings are missing; therefore your friends will consist mostly of women.

This completes this section of the Fortune. After a very little practice you will learn to interpret the different combinations of cards easily. After a little practice too, you will automatically memorize the meaning of all of the cards so you will not have to refer to the lists.

You may now gather up all of the cards and lay your chart to one side and prepare for the next layout which is very simple.

HOW TO TELL WHAT IS GOING TO HAPPEN TOMORROW

In this layout you will also need a chart at first. Later you will memorize it and then you may discard it.

On a piece of cardboard draw five squares, approximately 4 inches long and 3 inches wide. Arrange them in this position:

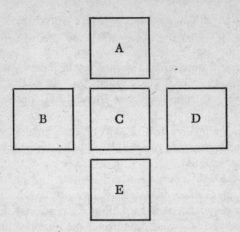

Square A represents the time around breakfast or from approximately 6 A.M. to 9:30 A.M.

Square B represents the time before lunchtime or from approximately 9:30 A.M. until noon.

Square C represents the afternoon or from approximately noon to 3:30 P.M.

Square D represents the time before supper or from approximately 3:30 P.M. until 6:30 P.M.

Square E represents the evening hours or from approximately 6:30 P.M. to 10:30 P.M.

When you have this chart drawn you may enter the hours in the various squares, which will be easier than referring to this list. After some practice you will automatically memorize the hours covered by each of the squares.

We are now ready for the next simple procedure. By learning each step thoroughly as you go along you will find that telling fortunes is very simple and accurate.

Lay the part of the deck of cards aside that you used in the first layout. Pick up the part of the deck that you discarded when you began the Fortune. The part of the deck that you use now has all of the 2, 3, 4, 5, and 6 sorts in it, but does not contain any of the cards you formerly used.

Shuffle the cards thoroughly. Then lay them on the table in front of you in a fan shape, with their faces down. Draw or choose five cards at random from them, and lay them in the squares on your chart in this manner:

Place the first card you choose in Square A, face up. Place the 2nd card you choose, face up in Square B. Place the 3rd chosen card in Square C; place the 4th chosen card in Square D—all of them face up. Now place the 5th chosen card in Square E, face down. The idea of placing this last card face down is just to create a bit of anxiety about how the day will terminate after you see what is going to happen for every other part of the day. When you have looked up the cards for the other portions of the day you may turn the card in Square E up and see what the evening hours have in store for you.

Meanings of the Cards in This Layout

HEARTS

TWO SPOT:	A medium-blond young man.
THREE SPOT:	A medium-light elderly man.
FOUR SPOT:	A medium-light lady.
FIVE SPOT:	Love. Affection. Good news. Happy frame of mind.
SIX SPOT:	Favors or a gift from a close friend or one of the family.

DIAMONDS

TWO SPOT:	Very good news by letter, telephone or messenger.

THREE SPOT: You will do some shopping or spend
                some money.

FOUR SPOT: You will be paid or will receive
                some money.

FIVE SPOT: You will sign some papers or make
                a promise.

SIX SPOT: You will make an important discov-
                ery or find a lost article.

CLUBS

TWO SPOT: A medium-dark young man.
THREE SPOT: A medium-dark elderly man.
FOUR SPOT: A medium-brunette lady.
FIVE SPOT: A favorable proposition.
SIX SPOT: Opportunity to take a favorable
                trip.

SPADES

TWO SPOT: Disappointment in some personal
                plans.

THREE SPOT: Loss of money or other valuables
                through carelessness.

FOUR SPOT: Some extra expenses. You will have
                to spend money.

FIVE SPOT: You will hear of some sickness or a
                minor accident.

SIX SPOT: You will feel irritable or cross and
                be impatient and restless.

SAMPLE OF "WHAT'S GOING TO HAPPEN TOMORROW" FORTUNE

For this example, lay the cards in the Squares as fol-

lows so that you may see them in front of you and follow the interpretation carefully:

In Square A, place the 4 of Spades.
In Square B, place the 6 of Hearts.
In Square C, place the 2 of Hearts.
In Square D, place the 5 of Diamonds.
In Square E, place the 2 of Clubs, face down.

This sample layout is supposed to be the cards you
have chosen after they have been shuffled, as instructed
previously.

We now begin the translation of this layout. Start
with Square A, at the top. Between 6 A.M. and 9:30
A.M., you will have to pay out some money that you
had probably not figured on. You may feel impelled to
say something disagreeable—this may leave a sort of
"bad taste" in your mouth so early in the morning, but
it will not be important. This is where you bring into
play any "hunches" or impressions that you may get
when reading the Fortune.

Then between 9:30 A.M. and noon, according to
Square B, you will have some favors conferred upon
you by close friends or relatives which will make you
very happy indeed.

In Square C, it says that between noon and 3:30
P.M. you will meet, or have some dealings or association with a medium-light man. The cards on either side
are red, which is good; therefore we will say that the
association will be agreeable. If they had been black,
then the association would not have amounted to much.

In Square D, we find that between 3:30 P.M. and
6:30 P.M. you will be concerned about some papers or
documents or if not, that you will make some agree-
ments or promises that will result favorably since there
is a red card to the left of it.

Now turn the card in Square E face up, which in

this example would be the 2 of clubs. This denotes that after supper or between 6:30 and 10:30 P.M. you will be with a medium-dark young man. If the one who is having the fortune told is a young lady, she may be told that this dark, handsome young man will take her somewhere or that she will have the opportunity to have a date with him. But if the person having their fortune told is a man, then he can be told that he will have the company of a young lady during the evening. In either case, the association will be pleasant because there is a red card above it.

Now we count the red cards and discover that there are more red cards than there are black cards. The day, therefore, will be a fortunate day for you, and you can safely go ahead and carry out any plans you might have.

However, if there should have been a majority of black cards the day would be rather unfavorable and you should postpone important plans until another time.

If all of the cards are red it will be a most successful day to push every interest and get as much accomplished as possible.

If all of the cards are black it will be a rather unsettled day and you should be careful to avoid accidents —guard your health and do not take any risks.

If there is a majority of hearts you will feel romantic during the day.

If there is a majority of diamonds you will be very much concerned about your home or personal affairs.

If there should be two of one suit and two of another suit, your thought and time will be equally divided between the two during the day.

With only a little practice you will be able to read these cards easily and rapidly. Remember to include your hunches.

HOW TO ANSWER QUESTIONS WITH CARDS

Almost everyone who has his Fortune told will have several questions come to mind that may be suggested by some of the things in the Fortune. It is very easy to answer questions with this system of fortune telling by cards.

To begin with, you must word your question so that it may be answered "Yes" or "No." Almost any question that may come to a person's mind can be worded in such a manner that it can be answered by "Yes" or "No."

The person asking the question must shuffle the cards thoroughly and while shuffling them must silently ask the question and keep his mind on that question while he is shuffling.

When answering questions you will remove all of the Face cards from the deck and lay them to one side.

After you have shuffled the number cards and asked the question, you will begin dealing the cards off from the back and turning them face up, four at a time. If an Ace does not appear with the first 4 cards dealt off, lay them to one side and deal off four more. When the first Ace appears, lay the 4 cards in front of you side by side on the table face up. Continue until all Four Aces are on the table in front of you. You now count the number of black spots, including the Aces. Then count the number of red spots, including the Aces. If there is a larger number of black spots, the answer is "No." If there is the larger number of red spots, the answer is "Yes."

If you have another question to ask put the cards back together, shuffle them and concentrate upon the question and go through the same laying-out process again.

As to how long you should shuffle the cards, let your "conscience" be your guide. You will have a "certain feeling" when you have shuffled them enough. Follow this feeling. Keep on shuffling them until something inside of you tells you that you have shuffled them sufficiently, then lay them out as per the above directions. This "inner feeling" is what one may call the "Voice of Fate" assuring you that you have shuffled them enough and that the cards are now in the right position to answer your questions accurately. When you have finished shuffling them, if you have a feeling that the deck should be cut once, twice or three times, do so—for this cutting may be necessary to get the cards in the proper position to the Aces to accurately answer your question.

You will perhaps by now realize that the "Secret" of telling fortunes by the Karma System is not in the Cards themselves, but is instead in the position of them according to the Karma interpretations. The cards are placed in their proper positions according to fate, by the "Conscience Shuffle"; that is, by shuffling them until your conscience tells you to stop, and the value of this System is also enhanced by adding to the regular interpretations any "hunches" or "impressions" that you may receive as you go along in the process of interpreting the cards.

SPECIAL NOTICE

NO ONE SHOULD TELL HIS FORTUNE BY CARDS, NOR HAVE HIS FORTUNE TOLD WITH THE CARDS MORE THAN ONCE EVERY 24 HOURS!

If you tell your fortune or have it told more than once in 24 hours, the fortunes will conflict. Two readings within 24 hours will neutralize the indications of both and you have not then had your Fortune told at all, but have been merely playing with the cards and cannot take what they tell you seriously.

Many people like to "run the cards" a second time, just to see if they will tell them the same thing again. This is an acknowledgement of your disbelief, which is resented by "Karma." Be satisfied with the first layout, take it seriously and you will be surprised at the accuracy of the predictions, provided you have followed the instructions correctly.

HOW TO FIND INITIALS OF FUTURE HUSBAND OR WIFE

This is a feature that many young people are very interested in. Also many persons want to learn if they will marry again, and if so, what the initials will be. First they should ask the cards if they will marry again. If the answer is "Yes" then they may proceed to find the initials of the next husband or wife. If the answer is "No," it will be useless to proceed.

THE ALPHABET IN THE CARDS

There are always 2 cards that represent each letter of the alphabet, a "blond" and a "brunette." A list of the letters and corresponding cards follow:

A—Ace of Hearts or Spades.
B—Two of Hearts or Spades.
C—Three of Hearts or Spades.
D—Four of Hearts or Spades.
E—Five of Hearts or Spades.
F—Six of Hearts or Spades.
G—Seven of Hearts or Spades.

H—Eight of Hearts or Spades.
I—Nine of Hearts or Spades.
J—Ten of Hearts or Spades.
K—Jack of Hearts or Spades.
L—Queen of Hearts or Spades.
M—King of Hearts or Spades.
N—Ace of Diamonds or Clubs.
O—Two of Diamonds or Clubs.
P—Three of Diamonds or Clubs.
Q—Four of Diamonds or Clubs.
R—Five of Diamonds or Clubs.
S—Six of Diamonds or Clubs.
T—Seven of Diamonds or Clubs.
U—Eight of Diamonds or Clubs.
V—Nine of Diamonds or Clubs.
W—Ten of Diamonds or Clubs.
X—Jack of Diamonds or Clubs.
Y—Queen of Diamonds or Clubs.
Z—King of Diamonds or Clubs.

HOW TO PROCEED

Shuffle the cards thoroughly and lay them out on the table in front of you, backed up in a "fan shape."

Now let your hand be directed by your "conscience." Choose one of the cards and take it out of the deck. Lay it face up, to your left. This is the Initial of your future husband's or wife's first name. Next draw another card and place it face up beside the first one, to its right. This is the initial of the middle name. Now let your hand be guided again in selecting the third and last card and place it face up to the right of the 2nd card. Now look in the list to see what letters the cards signify and discover the three initials of your future husband or wife. If you have followed your "conscience" in choosing these cards, they will be reasonably accurate.

If two of the cards are black and one red, the person will be a brunette. If two are red and one black the person will be a blond. If all black it will be a dark brunette.

CAUTION: You should never ask the cards to choose the initials of your future husband or wife more than once, unless they tell you that you are to be married more than once. Once you have been given the initials, write them down and remember them.

However, this system may be used over and over again to tell you the initials of your next new friend, new neighbors, next business partner, next employer, etc. Remember the cards deal with future associates, not past or present ones.

SECURING QUICK ANSWERS TO QUESTIONS

Shuffle all the cards thoroughly while you are silently asking the question. Cut the cards once and note if a red or black card turns up. Repeat the shuffling and cutting three times. If two out of the three cuts are red the answer is "Yes." However, if two of the three cuts are black cards the answer is "No." If all three cuts are red—the answer is "absolutely Yes." If the three cuts are all black, the answer is "positively No."

LEARNING THE NAME OF A CITY OR STATE

Shuffle the cards and spread them before you in a "fan" shape and carefully select 10 cards. Look up the letters that these 10 cards represent in the preceding Table. Now by rearranging these letters and changing them around, you will find that they almost spell a certain State or City. The City or State that they come the nearest spelling is the one you will likely visit on your trip.

HOW TO TELL HOW MANY CHILDREN YOU WILL HAVE

Remove all of the Face Cards from the deck. Shuffle the cards thoroughly, and cut them three times, shuffling them for each cut. Write down the number of the card you cut each time. Thus: If the Six of Diamonds was the first cut, write down 6. If the Ace of Clubs was the second cut, write down 1. If the 4 of Diamonds was the third cut, write down 4. Now total these numbers, which in this case is 12 and divide them by 3, which in this case is 4. You will likely have 4 children. If your sum is indivisible by 3, use the nearest number and discard the remainder. This way, if the total of your three cuts should be 11, we find that 3 will go into 11 only three times with a remainder of 2. We discard the 2 ond say you will have 3 children.

HOW TO TELL A PERSON'S AGE WITH THE CARDS

Use a deck of ordinary Playing Cards for this purpose and prepare it in advance, after which you may use it over and over.

Pick out of the deck the Ace, 2, 3, 4, 5, 6, and 7 of Diamonds, Clubs and Hearts. Across the tops of the cards write the following numbers:

Ace of Hearts:	8	29	50
2 Ace of Hearts:	9	30	51
3 Ace of Hearts:	10	31	52
4 Ace of Hearts:	11	32	53
5 Ace of Hearts:	12	33	54

6 Ace of Hearts:	13	34	55
7 Ace of Hearts:	14	35	56
Ace of Clubs:	15	36	57
2 Ace of Clubs:	16	37	58
3 Ace of Clubs:	17	38	59
5 Ace of Clubs:	18	39	60
4 Ace of Clubs:	19	40	61
6 Ace of Clubs:	20	41	62
7 Ace of Clubs:	21	42	63
Ace of Diamonds:	22	43	64
2 Ace of Diamonds:	23	44	65
3 Ace of Diamonds:	24	45	66
4 Ace of Diamonds:	25	46	67
5 Ace of Diamonds:	26	47	68
6 Ace of Diamonds:	27	48	69
7 Ace of Diamonds:	28	49	70

Shuffle these 21 cards and lay them face up on the table in three rows of 7 each. Let them overlap each other in each row but leave enough of the top of each card showing so the numbers are visible. Ask a person to tell you which row the card is in which has his or her age written on it. When they tell you which row it is in, pick up the three rows one at a time but put the row just indicated in the middle. Proceed to lay them out in the same manner again without shuffling them. Ask them to point out the row this time that the card is in. When they have done so put that row in the center, and deal them out once more. This time also put that row in the center. Now take up the deck and deal off 10 cards from either the top or the bottom, then look at the 11th card. The 11th card will be the one containing their age. You will be able to tell by looking at the person, which one of the three numbers is his age, since there is enough difference in the numbers to tell if a person is 8, 29, or 59 years of age; and the same for the rest of the numbers.

You will note of course that the range of ages is from 8 to 70. It is quite unlikely that you will have anyone younger than 8 or older than 70 to work with.

If you have made no mistake in laying out these cards and placing the proper row in the center each time, it will automatically work out that the 11th card is always the one containing the person's age. You can make yourself very popular among your friends by telling their ages in this manner, if you do not reveal the secret of the center row and the 11th card to them. Practice this with yourself until you become thoroughly familiar with the principle before attempting to do it for someone else.

THE MODERN SYSTEM

SIGNIFICATION OF THE 52 CARDS

The following definitions are based upon one of the oldest authorities dealing with the subject, and amplified by some of the more modern meanings now in vogue.

HEARTS

Ace—An important card, whose meaning is affected by its environment. Among hearts it implies love, friendship, and affection; with diamonds, money and news of distant friends; with clubs, festivities, and social or domestic rejoicing; with spades, disagreements, misunderstandings, contention, or misfortune; individually, it stands for the house.

King—A good-hearted man, with strong affections, emotional, and given to rash judgments, possessing more zeal than discretion.

Queen—A fair woman, loving and lovable, domesticated, prudent and faithful.

Knave—Not endowed with any sex. Sometimes taken as Cupid; also as the best friend of the inquirer, or as a fair person's thoughts. The cards on either side of the knave are indicative of the good or bad nature of its intentions.

Ten—A sign of good fortune. It implies a good heart, happiness, and the prospect of a large family. It counteracts bad cards and confirms good ones in its vicinity.

Nine—The wish card. It is the sign of riches, and of high social position accompanied by influence and esteem. It may be affected by the proximity of bad cards.

Eight—The pleasures of the table, convivial society. Another meaning implies love and marriage.

Seven—A faithless, inconstant friend who may prove an enemy.

Six—A confiding nature, liberal, open-handed, and an easy prey for swindlers; courtship, and a possible proposal.

Five—Causeless jealousy in a person of weak, unsettled character.

Four—One who has remained single till middle life from being too hard to please.

Three—A warning card as to the possible results of the inquirer's own want of prudence and tact.

Deuce—Prosperity and success in a measure dependent on the surrounding cards; endearments and wedding bells.

DIAMONDS

Ace—A ring or paper money.

King—A fair man, with violent temper and vindictive, obstinate turn of mind.

Queen—A fair woman given to flirtation, fond of society and admiration.

Knave—A near relative who puts his own interests first, is self-opinionated, easily offended and not always quite straight. It may mean a fair person's thoughts.

Ten—Plenty of money, a husband or wife from the country and several children.

Nine—This card is influenced by the one accompanying it; if the latter is a court card, the person referred to will have his capacities negated by a restless, wandering disposition. It may imply a surprise connected with money; if in conjunction with the eight of spades it signifies crossed swords.

Eight—A marriage late in life, which will probably be somewhat checkered.

Seven—This card has various meanings. It cautions of the need for careful action. It may imply a decrease of prosperity. Another reading connects it with uncharitable tongues.

Six—An early marriage and speedy widowhood. A warning with regard to a second marriage is also indicated.

Five—To young married people this portends good children. In a general way it means unexpected news, or success in business enterprises.

Four—Breach of confidence. Troubles caused by inconstant friends, vexations and disagreeableness.

Three—Legal and domestic quarrels and probable unhappiness caused by wife's or husband's temper.

Deuce—An unsatisfactory love affair; sudden opposition from relatives or friends.

CLUBS

Ace—Wealth, a peaceful home, industry and general prosperity.

King—A dark man of upright, high-minded nature, calculated to make an excellent husband, faithful and true in his affections.

Queen—A dark woman, with a trustful, affectionate disposition, with great charm for the opposite sex, and susceptible to male attractions.

Knave—A generous, trusty friend, who will take trouble on behalf of the inquirer. It may also mean a dark man's thoughts.

Ten—Riches suddenly acquired, probably through the death of a relation or friend.

Nine—Friction through opposition to the wishes of friends.

Eight—Love of money and a passion for speculating.

Seven—Great happiness and good fortune. If troubles come they will be caused by one of the opposite sex to the inquirer.

Six—Success in business both for self and children.

Five—An advantageous marriage.

Four—A warning against falsehood and double-dealing.

Three—Two or possibly three marriages, with money.

Deuce—Care is needed to avert disappointment and avoid opposition.

SPADES

Ace—It may concern love affairs, or convey a warning that troubles await the inquirer through bad speculations or ill-chosen friends.

King—A dark man, ambitious and successful in the higher walks of life.

Queen—A widow of malicious and unscrupulous nature, fond of scandal and open to bribes.

Knave—A well-meaning, lazy person, slow in action though kindly in thought.

Ten—An evil omen; grief or imprisonment. Has power to detract from the good signified by cards near it.

Nine—An ill-fated card meaning sickness, losses, troubles and family dissensions.

Eight—A warning with regard to any enterprise in hand. This card close to the inquirer means evil; also opposition from friends.

Seven—Sorrow caused by the loss of a dear friend.

Six—Hard work brings wealth and rest after toil.

Five—Bad temper and a tendency to interfere in the inquirer, but happiness to be found in the chosen wife or husband.

Four—Illness and the need for great attention to business.

Three—A marriage that will be marred by the inconstancy of the inquirer's wife or husband, or a journey.

Deuce—A removal, or possibly death.

In connection with the foregoing detailed explanation of the meaning of each card in an ordinary pack, we append a short table which may be studied either separately or with the preceding definitions.

It gives at a glance certain broad outlines which may be of use to one who wishes to acquire the art of reading a card as soon as it is laid face up.

A SHORT TABLE

PRUDENCE
Ace of clubs
6 of spades

WEALTH
9 of hearts
2 of hearts
7 of clubs
10 of diamonds
10 of clubs

REJOICING
8 of hearts

EARLY MARRIAGE
2 of clubs
6 of diamonds

3 of clubs
5 of clubs

LATE MARRIAGE
8 of diamonds
3 of clubs

PROSPERITY
10 of hearts
2 of hearts
7 of clubs
6 of clubs

PRESAGES
MISFORTUNE
10 of spades
9 of spades

8 of spades   2 of diamonds
7 of spades   2 of clubs
3 of spades   4 of spades
2 of spades
3 of diamonds   JEALOUSY
9 of clubs   5 of hearts

CREDIBILITY   UNFAITHFULNESS
6 of hearts   King of diamonds
                             4 of diamonds
DISCRETION NEEDED 4 of clubs
3 of hearts   7 of hearts
7 of diamonds

INFORMATION FOR READING FORTUNES WITH 52 REGULAR PLAYING CARDS

The 52 cards are shuffled and cut into three piles face up, with the left hand toward the inquirer. Before starting the deal, select the card that represents the person whose fortune is being told. (See signification of the cards.) This card, representing the Inquirer, is not withdrawn but is shuffled with the pack.

Lay all the cards out, nine in a row, from right to left in six rows. Only seven cards will be in the sixth row. (To save space, overlap the cards in each row, leaving about one-third of each card uncovered.)

After all 52 cards have been dealt out in six rows, find the first Key Card by counting nine cards from right to left from Inquirer's card.

(If the Inquirer's card happens to be in the sixth row, you must count straight upward from the Inquirer's card to the top row, and then from right to left.)

When you come to the last card in a row, continue the count in the next row below, moving from left to right. Repeat this process until there are not enough cards left to count nine before coming back to the Inquirer's card. This locates the remaining Key Cards, which reveal the Inquirer's Fortune.

Three readings are required to complete telling a fortune. The First reading usually represents the Past, the Second the Present, while the Third reveals the Future.

The following example, using the Queen of Hearts as the inquirer's card, illustrates a typical reading. Lay out the following cards:

FIRST READING (The Past)

First Line: Seven of Clubs, Seven of Spades, King of Spades, Ace of Diamonds, Ace of Hearts, Jack of Clubs, Four of Hearts, Eight of Hearts, Jack of Spades.

Second Line: Two of Diamonds, Three of Diamonds, Two of Hearts, Six of Hearts, King of Diamonds, Five of Clubs, Two of Clubs, Five of Spades, Three of Hearts.

Third Line: Five of Hearts, Six of Diamonds, Four of Clubs, Queen of Clubs, Five of Diamonds, Three of Spades, King of Hearts, Four of Diamonds, Ten of Spades.

Fourth Line: Nine of Spades, Queen of Spades, Eight of Diamonds, Ace of Spades, Six of Clubs, Queen of Diamonds, King of Clubs, Jack of Hearts, Six of Spades.

Fifth Line: Ten of Diamonds, Eight of Clubs, Seven of Diamonds, Ace of Clubs, Nine of Diamonds, Nine of Clubs, Jack of Diamonds, Ten of Hearts, Ten of Clubs.

Sixth Line: Eight of Spades, Queen of Hearts, Seven of Hearts, Four of Spades, Three of Clubs, Two of Spades, Nine of Hearts.

After you have laid out the cards according to instructions, note where the inquirer's card is located, (should it be in the very last row, remember to count upward and over to the left from the top row). Count nine cards from the inquirer's card and mark the card on a piece of paper, or take the card out of the layout so that you can look up its meaning. Continue until there are no longer nine cards between the final count and the inquirer's card. Should the inquirer's card be the ninth card, eliminate the count. Remember there must be nine cards from or between each Key Card.

According to this example, the Key Cards would be—Jack of Clubs, Six of Hearts, Three of Spades, Ace of Spades, Nine of Clubs. Now refer to the signification of the cards and put down the meaning of each Key Card.

Jack of Clubs: A generous, trustworthy friend who will go out of his way to help the inquirer.

Six of Hearts: An early marriage and a speedy separation. A warning with regard to a second.

Three of Spades: A marriage that may be marred by infidelity or incompatibility, or a journey.

Ace of Spades: Concerns ill-fated love affairs, also trouble through speculation and ill-chosen companion.

Nine of Clubs: Friction and opposition to the wishes and advice of friends.

The interpretation of the above fortune would be: Should the Queen of Hearts represent an unmarried woman it would indicate a warning against an unhappy marriage which would bring displeasure to her friends and family. She will disregard the advice of a sincere friend or suitor and marry in haste, which may result in a speedy separation. Foolish speculations will also add to her sorrows. She can avoid this only by heeding the advice of a trusty friend.

Should the Queen of Hearts represent a married woman then the fortune would indicate that if the events have not already occurred, she must be careful not to give too much credence to the reports of doubtful friends and must guard her own conduct carefully.

Note: The cards must be reshuffled between each reading, but for the purpose of this lesson we will pick up the cards in suits and lay them out as follows:

THE SECOND READING (The Present)

First Line: Eight of Clubs, Queen of Hearts, Six of Spades, Eight of Spades, Eight of Hearts, Six of Diamonds, Ten of Hearts, Nine of Clubs, Six of Hearts.

Second Line: Three of Spades, Ace of Spades, Three of Diamonds, King of Spades, Ace of Diamonds, Ace of Hearts, King of Diamonds, King of Clubs, Ace of Clubs.

Third Line: Ten of Spades, Five of Clubs, Two of Hearts, Five of Hearts, Ten of Diamonds, Four of Hearts, Two of Clubs, Jack of Spades, Three of Hearts.

Fourth Line: Five of Spades, Four of Clubs, Six of Clubs, Queen of Diamonds, Four of Diamonds, King of Hearts, Nine of Spades, Five of Diamonds, Seven of Clubs.

Fifth Line: Jack of Clubs, Ten of Clubs, Three of Clubs, Nine of Diamonds, Queen of Spades, Seven of Spades, Jack of Hearts, Eight of Diamonds, Seven of Diamonds.

Sixth Line: Seven of Hearts, Four of Spades, Queen of Clubs, Two of Spades, Jack of Diamonds, Two of Diamonds, Nine of Hearts.

When you have completed the layout, following previous instructions, the Key Cards will be the King of Clubs, Five of Clubs, Five of Diamonds, Ten of Clubs, Two of Diamonds and Three of Spades.

Referring to the signification of the Cards, we find:

King of Clubs: A dark upright man. An excellent husband, faithful and true.

Five of Clubs: An advantageous marriage.

Five of Diamonds: To young people this portends good children. In a general way it means unexpected good news or success in business.

Ten of Clubs: Riches suddenly acquired, possibly through the death of a relation or friend.

Two of Diamonds: An unsatisfactory love affair with opposition from relatives or friends.

Three of Spades: A marriage that will be marred by infidelity or incompatibility.

The definition of the above fortune would be: Should the Queen of Hearts be unmarried and young, then she would marry an upright dark man who will make an excellent husband. They will have good children and may receive a gift or legacy of a considerable sum of money. Should she be a married woman it would indicate an unsatisfactory love affair, marred by infidelity and incompatibility, notwithstanding the receipt of a legacy. It could also mean a second marriage would prove to be happy and successful, with financial security.

After picking up the suits, lay the cards out again for the third reading.

THE THIRD READING (The Future)

First Line: Ace of Clubs, Eight of Clubs, Queen of Hearts, Ten of Spades, King of Clubs, Five of Diamonds, Ten of Clubs, Nine of Spades, Jack of Spades.

Second Line: Three of Spades, Two of Spades, Six of Hearts, Eight of Spades, Five of Spades, Jack of Clubs, Seven of Hearts, Four of Spades, Queen of Clubs.

Third Line: Five of Hearts, Two of Diamonds, Three of Diamonds, Queen of Diamonds, Eight of Hearts, Three of Clubs, Ace of Diamonds, Six of Diamonds.

Fourth Line: Four of Diamonds, Six of Clubs, Seven of Diamonds, Seven of Clubs, Six of Spades, Seven of Clubs, Seven of Diamonds, Six of Spades, Nine of Diamonds, Jack of Diamonds, Nine of Hearts, Eight of Diamonds.

Fifth Line: Ten of Hearts, King of Spades, Two of Hearts, Ten of Diamonds, Ace of Hearts, Four of Hearts, King of Hearts, King of Diamonds, Queen of Spades.

Sixth Line: Two of Clubs, Seven of Spades, Jack of Hearts, Nine of Clubs, Three of Hearts, Four of Clubs, Ace of Spades.

When you complete this layout you will have the following Key Cards: Seven of Hearts, Three of Diamonds, Jack of Diamonds, Two of Hearts, Three of

Hearts and Ace of Clubs. Referring to the signification of the cards we find:

Seven of Hearts: A faithless, inconstant friend who may prove an enemy.

Three of Diamonds: Legal and domestic quarrels and unhappiness caused by bad tempers.

Jack of Diamonds: A male relative who puts his own interests first.

Two of Hearts: Endearments and wedding bells.

Three of Hearts: A warning card to the inquirer, who lacks prudence and tact.

Ace of Clubs: Wealth, a peaceful home, industry and general prosperity.

This fortune again warns the inquirer about the possibilities of disaster in marital and business affairs unless good judgment and careful consideration is given in dealing with friends and associates. It points out the pitfalls and dangers, as well as the rewards and good fortune, if the inquirer will heed the warnings and advice given.

Study this example carefully. Make up your own definitions, using the cards in this example. After a little practice you will become a proficient Fortune Teller.

A SIMPLE METHOD

THE PAST—PRESENT—FUTURE WITH THE
REDUCED DECK OF 32 CARDS

There is a very simple and generally accepted method of studying the past, the present and the future in the light of cartomancy. The selected pack of thirty-two cards from the sevens to the aces is required, and they must be shuffled and cut in the ordinary way. After the cut, the packs must not be placed one upon the other until the top card of the lower one and the bottom card of the upper one have been set aside to form the surprise. The remaining thirty cards are then to be dealt into three equal packs which, beginning at the left, represent respectively the Past, the Present and the Future.

We will suppose that the knave of hearts, a pleasure-seeking young bachelor, is the inquirer.

SIGNIFICATION OF THE CARDS

The individual meaning attached to the thirty-two cards employed is as follows:—

THE EIGHT CLUBS

Ace of Clubs—Signifies money, joy or good news; if reversed, the joy will be of brief duration.

King of Clubs—A frank, liberal man, fond of serving

his friends; if reversed he will meet with a disappointment.

Queen of Clubs—A clever and enterprising young man; reversed, a heartless flirt and flatterer.

The Knave of Clubs—A fair young man, possessed of no delicacy of feeling, who seeks to injure.

Ten of Clubs—Fortune, success or grandeur; reversed, want of success in some small matter.

Nine of Clubs—Unexpected gain, or a legacy; reversed, some trifling present.

Eight of Clubs—A dark person's affections, which, if returned, will be the cause of great prosperity; reversed, those of a fool, and attendant unhappiness if reciprocated.

Seven of Clubs—A small sum of money or unexpectedly recovered debt; reversed, a yet smaller amount.

THE EIGHT HEARTS

Ace of Hearts—A love letter, or some pleasant news; reversed, a friend's visit.

King of Hearts—A fair, liberal man; reversed, will meet with disappointment.

Queen of Hearts—A mild amiable woman; reversed, has been crossed in love.

Knave of Hearts—A gay, young bachelor who dreams only of pleasure; reversed, a discontented military man.

Ten of Hearts—Happiness, triumph; if reversed, some slight anxiety.

Nine of Hearts—Joy, satisfaction, success; reversed, a passing chagrin.

Eight of Hearts—A fair person's affections; reversed, indifference on his or her part.

Seven of Hearts—Pleasant thoughts, tranquility; reversed, ennui, weariness.

THE EIGHT DIAMONDS

Ace of Diamonds—A letter, soon to be received; reversed, containing bad news.

King of Diamonds—A fair man, generally in the army, but both cunning and dangerous; if reversed, a threatened danger caused by machinations on his part.

Queen of Diamonds—An ill-bred, scandal-loving woman; if reversed, she is to be greatly feared.

Knave of Diamonds—A tale-bearing servant, or unfaithful friend; if reversed, will be the cause of mischief.

Ten of Diamonds—Journey, or change of residence; if reversed, it will not prove fortunate.

Nine of Diamonds—Annoyance, delay; if reversed, either a family or a love quarrel.

Eight of Diamonds—Love-making; if reversed, unsuccessful.

Seven of Diamonds—Satire, mockery; reversed, a foolish scandal.

N.B.—In order to know whether the Ace, Ten, Nine, Eight and Seven of Diamonds are reversed, it is better to make a small pencil mark on each to show which is the top of the card.

THE EIGHT SPADES

Ace of Spades—Pleasure; reversed, grief, bad news.

King of Spades—The envious man, an enemy, or a dishonest lawyer who is to be feared; reversed, impotent malice.

Queen of Spades—A dark, ill-bred young man; reversed, he is plotting some mischief.

Queen of Spades—A widow; reversed, a dangerous and malicious woman.

Knave of Spades—A dark, ill-bred young man; reversed, he is plotting some mischief.

Ten of Spades—Tears, a prison; reversed, brief affliction.

Nine of Spades—Tidings of a death; if reversed, it will be some near relative.

Eight of Spades—Approaching illness; reversed, a marriage broken off, or offer refused.

Seven of Spades—Slight annoyance; reversed, a foolish intrigue.

The Court cards of Hearts and Diamonds usually represent persons of fair complexion; Clubs and Spades the opposite.

SIGNIFICATION OF DIFFERENT CARDS OF THE SAME DENOMINATION

Four Aces coming together, or following each other, announce danger, failure in business and sometimes imprisonment. If one or more of them are reversed, the danger will be lessened but that is all.

Three Aces coming in the same manner—Good tidings; if reversed, folly.

Two Aces—A plot; if reversed, will not succeed.

Four Kings—Rewards, dignities, honor; reversed, they will be less, but sooner received.

Three Kings—A consultation on important business, the result of which will be highly satisfactory; if reversed, success will be doubtful.

Two Kings—A partnership in business; if reversed, a dissolution of the same. Sometimes this only denotes friendly projects.

Four Queens—Company, society; one or more reversed denotes that the entertainment will not go off well.

Three Queens—Friendly calls; reversed, chattering and scandal, or deceit.

Two Queens—A meeting between friends; reversed, poverty, troubles, in which one will involve the other.

Four Knaves—A noisy party—mostly young people; reversed, a drinking bout.

Three Knaves—False friends; reversed, a quarrel with some low person.

Two Knaves—Evil intentions; reversed, danger.

Four Tens—Great success in projected enterprise; reversed, the success will not be so brilliant but still it will be sure.

Three Tens—Improper conduct; reversed, failure.

Two Tens—Change of trade or profession; reversed, denotes that the prospect is only a distant one.

Four Nines—A great surprise; reversed, a public dinner.

Three Nines—Joy, fortune, health; reversed, wealth lost by imprudence.

Two Nines—A little gain; reversed, trifling losses at cards.

Four Eights—A short journey; reversed, the return of a friend or relative.

Three Eights—Thoughts of marriage; reversed, folly, flirtation.

Two Eights—A brief love-dream; reversed, small pleasures and trifling pains.

Four Sevens—Intrigues among servants or low people, threats, snares, and disputes; reversed, their malice will be impotent to harm, and the punishment will fall on themselves.

Three Sevens—Sickness, premature old age; reversed, slight and brief indisposition.

Two Sevens—Levity; reversed, regret.

Any picture card between two others of equal value

—as two tens, two Aces, etc.—denotes that the person represented by that card runs the risk of prison.

It requires no great effort to commit these significations to memory, but it must be remembered that they are but what the alphabet is to the printed book; a little attention and practice, however, will soon enable the learner to form these mystic letters into words, and words into phrases; to assemble these cards together, and read the events past and to come that their faces reveal.

There are several ways of doing this, but we will give them all, one after another, so as to afford our readers a choice of methods of delving into the future.

We will suppose that the Knave of hearts, a pleasure-seeking young bachelor, is the inquirer.

The ten cards representing the Past are as follows:—

> The queen of clubs, reversed.
> The king of diamonds, reversed.
> The ten of clubs, reversed.
> The nine of diamonds.
> The eight of clubs.
> The ace of diamonds, reversed.
> The ace of hearts, reversed.
> The queen of spades, reversed.
> The eight of diamonds.

There are three pairs among the ten. Two queens, both reversed, remind the inquirer that he has had to suffer from the consequences of his own actions. The two aces, also both reversed, refer to some partnership into which he entered with good intentions but which was doomed to failure. The two eights speak of his frivolous pleasures and countless evanescent love affairs.

WHAT THE CARDS SAY

We will now see what the cards have to say, taken in order. We begin with the queen of clubs, reversed—a dark woman tormented by jealousy, in which she was encouraged by the king of diamonds, reversed, who is a treacherous schemer, wishing no good to the inquirer. The ten of clubs tells of a sea voyage, and is followed by the nine of diamonds, showing that there were vexations and annoyances on that voyage. The eight of clubs speaks of the Inquirer's having engaged the affections of a dark woman, who would have contributed to his prosperity and happiness. The ace of diamonds, reversed, represents evil tidings that reached him in connection with the ace of hearts, reversed, which stands for a change of abode, and emanating from the knave of spades, reversed, a legal agent who was not to be trusted. There was also the queen of spades, a designing widow with whom he had, the eight of diamonds, certain love passages.

THE PRESENT

The ten cards in the center pack are as follows:—

Ace of spades, reversed.
Seven of diamonds.
Eight of hearts.
Queen of hearts.
Seven of hearts.
Queen of diamonds, reversed.
Nine of spades.
King of hearts, reversed.
Knave of hearts, reversed.
Ten of diamonds.

In this pack we have only two pairs, two sevens speaking of mutual love; and two queens, one being reversed, which suggests rivalry.

Taken in order, the pack reads thus:—

The ace of spades, reversed, speaks of sorrow in which he will be treated with a certain amount of heartless chaff and want of sympathy, as it is followed by the seven of diamonds. The eight of hearts tells us that he is entertaining thoughts of marriage with the queen of hearts, a fair, lovable girl; but the seven of hearts shows that he is very contented with his present condition and in no hurry to change it. He is amusing himself with the queen of diamonds, reversed, who is a born flirt but more spiteful than he suspects, and who is next to the worst card in the pack, the nine of spades, indicative of the harm she does to him, and the failure of his matrimonial plans. He is cut out by the king of hearts, who thus causes him a serious disappointment, and we see him, himself, reversed as the lover with a grievance; the last card is the ten of diamonds, so he has decided to ease his heartache by traveling.

THE FUTURE

This pack contains the following cards:—
  The knave of diamonds, reversed.
  The seven of clubs.
  The eight of spades, reversed.
  The seven of spades, reversed.
  The ten of spades.
  The nine of hearts.
  The king of clubs.
  The ten of hearts.
  The king of spades.
  The ace of clubs, reversed.

The presence of four spades foretells that trouble awaits our bachelor. We again have a pair of sevens but one is reversed, so he may expect deceit to be at work. The two tens promise him an unlooked-for stroke of luck to be met with in a new walk in life, while the two kings speak of cooperation in business, and of the success which will crown his upright and practical conduct. The wish card, the nine of hearts, and the ten of hearts in a great measure counteract the mischief represented by the spades.

The inquirer must beware of the knave of diamonds, reversed, who is a mischief maker, who will make use of the seven of clubs, trifling financial matters, either to break off an engagement or to cause an offer of marriage to be refused, as shown by the eight of spades, reversed. The chagrined lover will have recourse to silly strategems in his love-making, the seven of spades, reversed, and this error will cause him grief, even to the shedding of tears, the ten of spades. The wish card, the nine of hearts, however, brings him better luck in his love affairs through his trusty, generous friend, the king of clubs. His ill-fortune is further counteracted by the next card, the ten of hearts, which promises him prosperity and success. He will find an enemy in the king of spades, a dark widower who is a lawyer by profession, and none too scrupulous in his ways. He may expect a good deal of troublesome correspondence with this man, as shown by the last card, the ace of clubs, reversed.

The subject of this correspondence is possibly to be found in the surprise, which consists of the nine of clubs, reversed, meaning an unexpected acquisition of money under a will. He will do well to take heed when in the companionship of the knave of clubs, reversed, the second card of the surprise, for he is a flatterer and a somewhat irresponsible character.

DEALING THE CARDS BY THREES

Take the pack of thirty-two selected cards—viz. the
Ace, King, Queen, Knave, Ten, Nine, Eight, and Seven
of each suit, having decided upon the one intended to
represent the inquirer. In doing this, it is necessary to
remember that the card chosen should be according to
the complexion of the chooser: King or Queen of Diamonds for a very fair person, ditto of Hearts for one
rather darker, Clubs for the one darker still, and Spades
only for one very dark indeed. The card chosen also
loses its signification and simply becomes the representative of a dark or fair man or woman, as the case
may be.

This point having been settled, shuffle the cards and
either cut them or have them cut, taking care to use the
left hand. That done, turn them up by threes, and
every time there appears in these triplets two of the
same suit, such as two Hearts, two Clubs, etc., with-
draw the highest card and place it on the table. If the
triplet should be all of the same suit, the highest card
is the only one withdrawn; but should it consist of
three of the same value but different suits, such as
three Kings, etc., they are all to be appropriated. We
will suppose that after having turned up the cards
three by three, six had been withdrawn, leaving twen-
ty-six to be shuffled and cut, and again turned up by
threes as before, until either thirteen, fifteen, or seventeen cards have been obtained. Remember that the
number must always be uneven, and that the card representing the inquirer must be one of them. If the
requisite thirteen, fifteen, or seventeen have been obtained, and the inquirer's card has not made its appearance, the operation must be done over. Let us suppose
the inquirer is a lady, represented by the Queen of
Hearts, and that fifteen cards have been obtained and

laid out—in the form of a half circle—in the order they were drawn, viz., the Seven of Clubs, the Ten of Diamonds, the Seven of Hearts, the Knave of Clubs, the King of Diamonds, the Queen of Hearts, the Nine of Clubs, the Seven of Spades, the Ace of Clubs, the Eight of Spades. Having considered these cards and finding among them two Queens, two Knaves, two tens, three sevens, two eights, and two nines, the observation would go thus:

The two Queens signify the reunion of friends, the two Knaves that there is michief being made between them. The two tens denote a change of profession, which, from one of them being between two sevens, will not be made without some difficulty, the cause of which, according to the three sevens, will be illness. However, the two nines promise some small gain, resulting—so say the two eights—from a love affair.

Now begin to count seven cards from right to left, beginning with the Queen of Hearts, who represents the inquirer. The seventh being the King of Diamonds means the inquirer often thinks of a fair man in uniform.

The next seventh card (counting the King of Diamonds as one) proves to be the Ace of Clubs signifying receipt from him of some very joyful tidings; also he intends making the inquirer a present.

Count the Ace of Clubs as "one" and proceed to the next seventh card, the Queen of Spades . . . a widow is endeavouring to injure the inquirer on this very account; and (the seventh card, counting the Queen as one, being the Ten of Diamonds) this annoyance will oblige the inquirer either to take a journey or change residence; but (the Ten of Diamonds being imprisoned between two sevens) the journey or move will meet with some obstacle.

Counting as before, calling the Ten of Diamonds

one, the seventh card will prove to be the Queen of Hearts, the inquirer's card, and it may be safely concluded that the inquirer will overcome these obstacles without needing anyone's aid or assistance.

Now take the two cards at either end of the half-circle, which are, respectively, the Eight of Spades and the Seven of Clubs, unite them and they may be read as a sickness which will lead to the receipt of a small sum of money.

Repeat the same manoeuvre, which brings together the Ace of Clubs and the Ten of Diamonds: Good news which will make the inquirer decide to take a journey, destined to prove a very happy one, and which will occasion the receipt of a sum of money.

The next pair, the Seven of Spades and the Seven of Hearts, brings tranquility and peace of mind followed by slight anxiety but quickly succeeded by love and happiness.

Then come the Nine of Clubs and the Knave of Clubs, foretelling a certain receipt of money, through the exertions of a clever, dark young man—Queen of Hearts and King of Diamonds—which comes from the fair man in uniform; this announces great happiness in store, and complete fulfillment of wishes—Knave of Diamonds and Nine of Diamonds—although this happy result will be delayed for a time through a fair young man not famed for his delicacy. Eight of Hearts and Ten of Hearts—love, joy, and triumph. The Queen of Spades, who remains alone is the widow who is endeavoring to injure the inquirer, and who finds herself abandoned by her friends.

Now gather up the cards, shuffle and cut them with the left hand and proceed to make them into three packs by dealing one to the left, one in the middle, and one to the right; a fourth is laid aside to form "a surprise." Continue to deal the cards to each of the three packs in turn until their number is exhausted. It will be found that the left hand and middle pack each contain five cards while the one on the right hand has only four.

Now ask the inquirer to select one of the three packs. We will suppose this to be the middle one, and that the cards comprising it are the Knave of Diamonds, the King of Diamonds, the Seven of Spades, the Queen of Spades, and the Seven of Clubs. These, by recalling our previous signification of the cards, are easily interpreted as follows:—

"The Knave of Clubs—a fair young man of no delicacy of feeling who seeks to injure—the King of Diamonds—a fair man in uniform—Seven of Spades—and will succeed in causing him some annoyance—the Queen of Spades—at the instigation of a spiteful woman—Seven of Clubs—but, by means of a small sum of money, matters will finally be easily arranged."

Next take up the left-hand pack which is "for the house"—the former one having been for the inquirer. Supposing it to consist of the Queen of Hearts, the Knave of Clubs, the Eight of Hearts, the Nine of Diamonds and the Ace of Clubs, they would read thus:—

"Queen of Hearts—the inquirer is, or soon will be, in a house—Knave of Clubs—where she will meet a dark young man who—Eight of Hearts—will entreat her assistance to forward his interest with a fair girl—Nine of Diamonds—he having met with delays and disappointments—Ace of Clubs—but a letter will arrive announcing the possession of money which will remove all difficulties."

The third pack is "for those who did not expect it," and is composed of four cards, let us say the Ten of Hearts, Nine of Clubs, Eight of Spades, and Ten of Diamonds, signifying:—

"The Ten of Hearts—unexpected good fortune and

great happiness—Nine of Clubs—caused by an unlooked-for legacy—Eight of Spades—which may perhaps be followed by a slight sickness—Ten of Diamonds
—the result of a fatiguing journey."

There now remains on the table only the card intended for the "surprise." This, however, must be left
untouched, the other cards gathered up, shuffled, cut
and again laid out in three packs, not forgetting at the
first deal to add a card to "the surprise." After the different packs have been examined and explained they
must again be gathered up and shuffled, repeating the
whole operation, after which the three cards forming
"the surprise" are examined. Supposing them to be the
Seven of Hearts, the Knave of Clubs, and the Queen
of Spades, they are to be interpreted—

"Seven of Hearts—Pleasant thoughts and friendly intentions—Knave of Clubs—of a dark young man—related to a malicious dark woman or widow who will
cause him much unhappiness."

DEALING THE CARDS BY SEVENS

After having shuffled the pack of thirty-two selected
cards—which as we before stated, consists of the Ace,
King, Queen, Knave, Ten, Nine, Eight, and Seven of
each suit—either cut them, or let the inquirer cut them,
taking care to use the left hand. Then count seven
cards beginning with the one lying on the top of the
pack. The first six are useless, so put them aside and
retain only the seventh, which is placed face upwards
on the table. Repeat this three times more, then shuffle
and cut the cards that were thrown to one side together with those remaining in your hand, and deal
them out in sevens as before until twelve cards are obtained. It is, however, indispensable that the one representing the inquirer should be among the number;

therefore, the whole operation must be done again in case it doesn't make its appearance. The twelve cards, being now spread out in the order in which they have been dealt, the explanation may begin as described in the manner of dealing the cards in threes—always bearing in mind both their individual and relative signification. Count the cards first by sevens, beginning with the one representing the inquirer, going from right to left. Then take the two cards at either end of the line or half circle and unite them. Afterwards form the three heaps or packs and "the surprise" precisely as before. The only difference between the two methods is the manner in which the cards are obtained.

DEALING THE CARDS BY FIFTEENS

After having well shuffled and cut the cards, or as we have said before, had them cut, deal them out in two packs containing sixteen cards in each. Ask the inquirer to choose one of them, lay aside the first card to form "the surprise", turn up the other fifteen, and arrange them in a half circle from left to right, placing them in the order in which they come to hand, and taking care to notice whether the one representing the inquirer is among them. If not, the cards must be gathered up, shuffled, cut and dealt as before. This must be repeated until the missing card shows up in the pack chosen by the inquirer.

Now proceed to explain them—first by interpreting the meaning of any pairs, triplets or quartets among them; then by counting them in sevens going from right to left, and beginning with the card representing the inquirer, and finally, by taking the cards at either end of the line and pairing them. Then gather up the fifteen cards, shuffle them, cut and deal so as to form three packs each of five cards. From each of these three packs remove the topmost card, and place them on the one laid aside for "the surprise," thus forming four packs of four cards each.

Ask the inquirer to choose one of these packs "for herself" or "himself," as the case may be. Turn it up and spread out the four cards from left to right, explaining their individual and relative significance. Next proceed with the pack on the left which will be "for the house"; then the third one, "for those who do not expect it"; and lastly "the surprise."

In order to make our meaning perfectly clear we will give another example. Let us suppose that the pack for the inquirer is composed of the Knave of Hearts, the Ace of Diamonds, the Queen of Clubs, and the Eight of Spades reversed. With the aid of the list of meanings we have given, it will be easy to interpret them as follows:—

"The Knave of Hearts is a gay young bachelor—the Ace of Diamonds—who has written, or will very soon write a letter—the Queen of Clubs—to a dark woman—Eight of Spades reversed—to make a proposal to her which will not be accepted."

On looking back to the list of significations, it will be found to run thus:—

Knave of Hearts—A gay young bachelor who thinks only of pleasure.

Ace of Diamonds—A letter soon to be received.

Queen of Clubs—An affectionate woman but quick tempered and touchy.

Eight of Spades—If reversed, a marriage broken off or offer refused.

It will thus be seen that each card forms a phrase. These may be assembled with little practice to form complete sentences. Of this we will give a further example by interpreting the signification of the three other packs—"for the house," "for those who do not expect it," and "the surprise." The first of these, "for the house," we will suppose to consist of Queen of Hearts, the Knave of Spades reversed, the Ace of Culbs, and the Nine of Diamonds, which reads thus:—

"The Queen of Hearts is a fair woman, mild and amiable in disposition, who—Knave of Spades reversed —will be deceived by a dark, ill-bred young man—the Ace of Clubs—but she will receive some good news which will console her—Nine of Diamonds—although it is probable that the news may be delayed."

The pack "for those who do not expect it," consisting of the Queen of Diamonds, the King of Spades, the Ace of Hearts reversed, and the Seven of Spades, would signify:—

"The Queen of Diamonds is a michief-making woman—the King of Spades—is in league with a dishonest lawyer—Ace of Hearts reversed—they will hold a consultation together—Seven of Spades—but the harm they will do will soon be repaired."

Last comes "the surprise," formed by, we will suppose, the Knave of Clubs, the Ten of Diamonds, the Queen of Spades, and the Nine of Spades, of which the interpretation is:—

"The Knave of Clubs is a clever, enterprising young man—Ten of Diamonds—about to undertake a journey —Queen of Spades—for the purpose of visiting a widow —Nine of Spades—but one or both of their lives will be endangered."

THE TWENTY-ONE CARDS

After having shuffled the thirty-two cards, and cut, or had them cut with the left hand, deal from the pack the first eleven and lay them on one side. The remainder—twenty-one in all—are to be again shuffled and cut. That done, lay the topmost card on one side to form "the surprise," and range the remaining twenty before you, in the order in which they come to hand. Then see whether the card representing the inquirer is among them; if not, one must be withdrawn from the eleven useless ones, and placed at the right end of the row to represent the missing card, no matter what it may really be. We will, however, suppose that the inquirer is an officer in the army and is represented by the King of Diamonds, and that the twenty cards ranged before you are the Queen of Diamonds, the King of Clubs, the Ten of Hearts, the Ace of Spades, the Queen of Hearts reversed, the Seven of Spades, the Knave of Diamonds, the Ten of Clubs, the King of Spades, the Eight of Diamonds, the King of Hearts, the Nine of Clubs, the Knave of Spades reversed, the Seven of Hearts, the Ten of Spades, the King of Diamonds, the Ace of Diamonds, the Seven of Clubs, the Nine of Hearts, and the Ace of Clubs.

Proceed to examine the cards as they lie and seeing that all the four kings are there, it can be predicted that great rewards await the inquirer, and that he will gain great dignity and honor. The two queens, one of them reversed, announce the reunion of two sorrowful friends; the three aces foretell good news; the two knaves, one of them reversed, danger; the three tens, unchanged conduct.

Now begin to explain the cards, commencing with the first on the left hand, the Queen of Diamonds. "The Queen of Diamonds is a mischief-making, under-bred woman—the King of Clubs—endeavouring to win the affections of a worthy and estimable man—Ten of Hearts—over whose scruples she will triumph—Ace of Spades—the affair will make some noise—Queen of Hearts reversed—and greatly distress a charming, fair woman who loves him—Seven of Spades—but her grief will not be of long duration—Knave of Diamonds—an unfaithful servant—Ten of Clubs—will make off with a considerable sum of money—King of Spades—and will be brought to trial—Eight of Diamonds—but saved from punishment through a woman's agency. King of Hearts—a fair man of liberal disposition—Nine of Clubs —will receive a large sum of money—Knave of Spades reversed—which will expose him to the malice of a dark youth of coarse manners. Seven of Hearts—pleasant thoughts followed by—Ten of Spades—great chagrin— King of Diamonds—await a man in uniform, who is the inquirer—Ace of Diamonds—but a letter he will speedily receive—Seven of Clubs—containing a small sum of money—Nine of Hearts—will restore his good spirits— Ace of Clubs—which will be further augmented by some good news." Now turn up "the surprise." We will suppose it to prove the Ace of Hearts—"a card that predicts great happiness, caused by a love letter, but which by making up the four aces, shows that this sudden joy will be followed by great misfortune."

Now gather up the cards, shuffle, cut and form into three packs, laying one aside at the first deal to form "the surprise." By the time they are all dealt out it will be found that the two first packets are each composed of seven cards, while the third contains only six. Ask the inquirer to select one of these, take it up, and spread out the cards from left to right, explaining them as before described.

Gather up the cards again, shuffle, cut, form into three packs (dealing one card to the surprise) and proceed as before. Repeat the whole operation once more; then take up the three cards forming the surprise and give their interpretation.

We may remark that no matter how the cards are dealt, whether by threes, sevens, fifteens, or twenty-one, when those lower than the Knave predominate, it foretells success; if Clubs are the most numerous, they predict gain, considerable fortune; if picture cards, dignity and honor; Hearts, gladness, good news; Spades, death or sickness.

These significations are necessarily very vague, and must of course be governed by the positions of the cards.

A REDUCED PACK

AN EXAMPLE—THE THREE PACKS—
THE SURPRISE

This method requires a pack of thirty-two cards, although only twenty-one of them are actually used in the process. The whole pack must be well shuffled and cut with the left hand. The dealer then removes the first eleven cards and puts them aside. From the twenty-one left in his hand he takes the uppermost card and places it apart for "the surprise" before dealing out the other twenty and placing them in order on the table before him. If the card representing the inquirer is not among them the whole process must be repeated from the beginning.

The signification of the cards must be read, taking care to notice any set of two, three, or four of a kind, as their collective meaning should be added to the individual explanation. After this has been done the twenty cards should be taken in order starting from the left, and their meanings linked together as a continuous message.

The cards must now be taken up again, shuffled and cut as before. The dealer then makes them into three packs, having been careful to place the first card apart for "the surprise." Two of the packs will consist of seven cards, the third of only six.

The inquirer is then asked to choose one of the packs, which must be exposed face upwards, moving

from left to right, and these six or seven cards, as the
case may be, should be read according to their significations. This operation is repeated three times, so that
at the finish "the surprise" consists of three cards which
are exposed and read last of all.

AN EXAMPLE

The accompanying example will make the foregoing
explanation more lucid and interesting.

We will take the knave of clubs as the representative
of the inquirer, a dark, clever, well-intentioned young
man. The twenty-one cards come out in the following
order, beginning from the left:—

The king of spades.	Ten of spades.
Queen of hearts, reversed.	Ace of diamonds, reversed.
Ace of hearts.	King of diamonds.
Knave of clubs.	Seven of diamonds.
Ace of spades, reversed.	Eight of diamonds.
Ace of clubs.	Eight of spades.
Knave of hearts.	Seven of clubs, reversed.
King of hearts.	Nine of clubs, reversed.
Queen of spades, reversed.	Nine of diamonds.
Nine of hearts.	The surprise, placed apart.
Knave of diamonds.	

Before taking the individual significance of each
card we will look at some of the combinations. There
are the four aces telling of bad news, relating to trouble through the affections, but two being reversed miti-
gate the evil, and give a ray of hope to the inquirer.
The three kings tell of an important undertaking which
will be discussed and carried through successfully by
the young man, who has excellent abilities. The two
queens, both reversed, warn the inquirer that he will

suffer from the result of his own actions, more especially as the queen of spades in an inverted position represents a malicious and designing widow. It will be found
as the process develops that she is very much to the
fore with regard to the inquirer's affairs. The three
knaves confirm the foregoing reading, for they foretell
annoyances and worries from acquaintances, ending
even in slander. The three nines, one of them reversed,
speak of happiness and entire success in an undertaking, though the inversion shows that there will be a
slight passing difficuty to overcome. The two eights refer to flirtations on the part of the inquirer, and one
being reversed warns him that he will have to pay for
some of his fun. The two sevens tell of mutual love between the young man and the lady of his choice, but
as the one is reversed there will be deceit at work to
try and separate them.

Now let us see what the twenty cards have to say
taken consecutively. We start off with the king of
spades, a clever, ambitious but unscrupulous man who
has been instrumental in thwarting the love affairs of
the fair, lovable and tenderhearted woman, the queen
of hearts, upon whom the inquirer has set his affections. The ace of hearts following her is the love letter
she will receive from the inquirer, the knave of clubs;
but he is next to the ace of spades, reversed, foretelling
grief to him which may affect his health, and the ace of
clubs coming immediately after points to the cause being connected with money. The next three cards are
court cards and that means gaiety in which the inquirer will be mixed up with a lively young bachelor—
the knave of hearts—a fair, generous but hot-tempered
man—the king of diamonds—and the malicious, spiteful
widow represented by the queen of spades, reversed.
The inquirer will meet with pleasure caused by success, the nine of hearts; but this is closely followed by

the knave of diamonds, an unfaithful friend who will try to bring disgrace, the ten of spades, upon his betters, and will write a letter containing unpleasant news —the ace of diamonds, reversed—which will concern or be prompted by the king of diamonds, a military man who has a grievance with regard to his love affairs and who is not above having recourse to scandal, the seven of diamonds, to avenge his wounded vanity. The next card is the eight of diamonds, the sign of some love-making, but our young people are not at the end of their troubles yet, for the eight of spades, reversed, tells us that his offer of marriage will be rejected. The seven of clubs is a card of caution, and implies danger from the opposite sex, so we gather that the spiteful widow has been at work and is possibly to blame for his rejection; this idea is further strengthened by the nine of clubs, also reversed, coming immediately, which suggests letters that may have done the mischief. The nine of diamonds tells of the annoyance caused by these events and their effect upon the affections of a dark person, the inquirer, who is a man well worth having.

In the first deal the inquirer chooses the middle pack which contains the following cards: the knave of diamonds, the seven of diamonds, the ace of clubs, the queen of spades, reversed, the ace of spades, the ace of diamonds, the eight of diamonds.

We notice that three aces come out in this pack and show passing troubles in love affairs. The knave of diamonds, an unfaithful friend, is mixed up in scandal, the seven of diamonds, conveyed in a letter, the ace of clubs, written or instigated by the spiteful widow, the queen of spades. The ace of spades betokens sickness, but it is followed by the ace of diamonds, the wedding ring, and the pack closes with the eight of diamonds,

THE THREE PACKS

	One Chosen by Inquirer	

What the first selected pack contains—

Knave of Diamonds	Seven of Diamonds	Ace of Clubs	★ Queen of Spades ★

Ace of Spades	Ace of Diamonds	Eight of Diamonds

The three cards forming the surprise—

King of Spades	Queen of Hearts	★ Nine of Hearts ★

★ Means "reversed"

telling of a happy marriage for the inquirer after all his worries.

In the second deal he again selects the middle pack, and we see the following: the queen of spades, reversed as usual, the nine of clubs, reversed, the seven of clubs, reversed, the nine of hearts, the seven of diamonds, the eight of clubs, small worries, and two sevens, one reversed, which show there is deceit at work. The pack reads thus: the queen of spades, the spiteful widow, who seems to be ubiquitous, is followed by the nine of clubs, representing the letter referred to above and the seven of clubs standing next to it sounds a word of caution to the inquirer as to his lady.

There are two nines, one reversed, speaking of a friend, so-called; he will probably succeed in outwitting the widow, for the next card is the nine of hearts, implying joy and success in spite of scandal, the seven of diamonds, with reference to his affections, represented by the eight of clubs.

In the third deal the inquirer still is faithful to the middle pack, and we find the following cards: the ace of diamonds, ten of spades, reversed, queen of spades, reversed, nine of diamonds, reversed, seven of clubs, reversed, ace of clubs, reversed.

The two aces, one of them reversed, tell of a union between two parties, but as the colors cross and one is reversed the result will not be known at present. Here we get the wedding ring, the ace of diamonds, followed by the ten of spades, reversed, which speaks of brief sorrow, occasioned doubtless by the spiteful widow, who again appears reversed and intent upon mischief; next to her comes the nine of diamonds, reversed, signifying a love quarrel; the seven of clubs, reversed, gives a word of caution to the inquirer with regard to the opposite sex; the last card is the ace of clubs, reversed which means joy soon followed by sorrow.

It is remarkable that the queen of spades comes out in each of the packs and is reversed every time.

THE SURPRISE

The surprise is now turned up and contains the king of spades, a dark, ambitious, unscrupulous man who has interfered with the love affairs of the fair woman, the queen of hearts, to whom the inquirer has made an offer, so far without success; the third card is the nine of hearts, reversed, which tells that it will be but a passing cloud that will separate the lovers.

THE SEVEN PACKS METHOD

The seven packs represent respectively—"yourself," "your house," "what you expect," "what you don't expect," "a great surprise," "what is sure to come true," and "the wish."

The cards having been shuffled and cut once, and dealt out in the manner described, these are the combinations we get:—

First Pack—Queen of spades, queen of hearts, ten of clubs, seven of hearts.

Second—Ace of spades, knave of clubs, ace of diamonds, and ten of spades.

Third—Knave of spades, king of diamonds, knave of hearts.

Fourth—Queen of clubs, seven of spades, king of spades.

Fifth—Ten of diamonds, eight of clubs, and queen of diamonds.

Sixth—King of hearts, ten of hearts, king of clubs.

Wish—Ace of hearts, knave of diamonds, ace of clubs.

The first pack represents to me the meeting of the inquirer with a dark or elderly woman, for whom she has a strong affection. Water is crossed before that meeting takes place.

The second pack reads as if a dark man would offer a ring or a present of jewelry, and also that he is meditating a journey by land. He is probably a professional man, or in government service.

The third pack, with its combination of knaves and king, has reference to business transactions which will most probably be favorable to the interests of the queen.

The fourth pack presages some slight disappointment, illness or unhappiness in connection with some friends.

The fifth pack tells us that some brilliant fortune is awaiting a fair friend, which will lead to a higher social position.

The sixth pack tells us that perhaps our seemingly indifferent queen of hearts has a slight tenderness for some one. He is older than she is, and is only waiting for an opportunity to declare his affection. If the wish is related to such a man as I have described, she may be certain of its fulfillment, even should there be a slight delay.

The seventh or wish pack is extremely good, and tells us that many affairs will be transacted by writing.

The future of the queen of hearts is fair and bright, her disposition is lovable, and she will bring happiness to other people.

This example is not made up of selected cards. They were shuffled, cut and drawn in the ordinary way. I say this because so few cards of bad import have appeared, and it might be thought these were chosen in order to avoid prophesing disappointments.

In the foregoing example twenty-three cards were dealt out, but the number may vary. It must, however, be an uneven number. Sometimes only fifteen or seventeen cards are taken, and with the smaller quantity of selected cards there is an optional way of concluding operations. After having read the pairs, the cards are gathered up, shuffled and cut into three packs instead of seven. These three are placed in a row, and a fourth card is put aside for the surprise. The inquirer is requested to choose one of the three packs, which represent respectively, For the house, For those who did not expect it, and For the inquirer—the last being decided by the choice of the person in question.

When these three packs have been read, all the cards are again taken up except the Surprise (which is left face downwards on the table), and dealt out again, the same process is repeated three times until there are three cards set aside for the surprise. These are read last of all and form the concluding message to the inquirer. Let's hope it may be a cheerful one!

GYPSY METHOD

General outline—Signification of cards—How to consult the cards—An illustration—Its reading.

Here again the pack of thirty-two cards is used, the cards from two to six inclusive being discarded.

GENERAL OUTLINE

The general meaning pertaining to each suit is as follows: The court cards bear the signification of people, and the king, queen, and knave in each suit suggest relationship. The kings indicate the profession followed.

Thus, the king of spades denotes a literary man, or one whose ambition would lead him to the pulpit or the platform.

The king of hearts is the symbol of a wealthy man —one who deals with large sums of money—for instance, a banker, capitalist, or stockholder.

The king of clubs indicates the mental side of business, and here we look for the lawyer or attorney.

The king of diamonds is a businessman—one who depends on both his brain and hands for work. Diamonds are eminently the practical suit, and must always be consulted with reference to the subject's condition in life. They signify the material side of life so this suit indicates success, or the absence of it— failure.

There is a very slight variation in the signification of the cards from that given in the preceding method, but it is well to observe it carefully as the mode of procedure is entirely different.

SIGNIFICATION OF CARDS

HEARTS

Ace . . . Quietness and domestic happiness.
Seven . . . Love.
Eight . . . A surprise.
Nine . . . A wish.
Ten . . . A wedding.

SPADES

Ace . . . Government service.
Reverse Ace . . . A death.
Seven . . . Unpleasant news.
Eight . . . Sorrow or vexation.
Nine . . . Quarrels.
Ten . . . A disappointment.

DIAMONDS

Ace . . . A letter or ring.
Seven . . . A journey.
Eight . . . Society.
Nine . . . Illness, or news of a birth.
Ten . . . Money, joy, success.

CLUBS

Ace . . . A present.
Seven . . . Gain, good business.
Eight . . . Pleasure.
Nine . . . A proposal.
Ten . . . A journey by water.

HOW TO CONSULT THE CARDS

The inquirer is to shuffle the pack of cards and cut it into three. Take up the cards and let your subject draw any chance card that he pleases. Place this card on the table. The suit from which it is drawn will determine the representative card as it is an indication of the character of your subject.

A lady is represented by a queen, a man by a king, and the knave stands for the male relations or thoughts.

After the card is drawn, place the remainder on the table in four rows, beginning each row from left to right.

The cards that immediately surround the king or queen aid us in our judgment of the inquirer—remember that the right-hand card is the more important one.

AN ILLUSTRATION

A practical illustration will explain my meaning, and again we will suppose a lady has cut the cards to have her fortune read.

The cards being shuffled and cut into three, the card was drawn, and as this proved to be a seven of clubs, so the queen represented the subject in this instance. When the cards were placed in order, this is how they appeared.

First line—Seven of clubs, eight of clubs, king of clubs, seven of hearts, king of diamonds, nine of diamonds, ten of diamonds, king of hearts.

Second line—Seven of spades, nine of spades, knave of hearts, king of spades, eight of spades, queen of spades, ten of spades, ace of diamonds.

Third line—Ace of spades, knave of clubs, queen of

clubs, ten of hearts, ace of hearts, queen of diamonds, ace of clubs, nine of hearts.

Fourth line—Knave of spades, seven of diamonds, eight of hearts, nine of clubs, eight of diamonds, knave of diamonds, queen of hearts, ten of clubs.

ITS READING

Now we can proceed with the reading:—

As the suit of clubs is a pleasant one, we may conclude the lady is of a cheerful temperament. The seven itself signifies gain and prosperity, and the eight pleasure, which come to the inquirer through the king of clubs—typical of a lawyer. The seven of hearts indicates that a fair man is in love with the inquirer. The nine of diamonds, with the joyful ten beside it, seems to foretell a birth, and the king of hearts stands for a good friend. But the seven and nine of spades, in conjunction, inform us that some annoyance is coming which is possibly connected with the king of hearts.

The king of spades, accompanied by the eight of that suit, tells that this man is suffering considerable grief and vexation on account of the queen of clubs, suffering which will cause another woman to be jealous.

The queen and ten of spades, with the ace of spades, imply disagreeable tidings; but as the knave of clubs appears side by side with the queen of that suit (the inquirer), and they are followed by the ten of hearts, it will in no way disturb the affection of either. The knave here may be taken to indicate the thoughts or intentions of the king. The ace of hearts seems to promise great tranquility and happiness in the domestic life. A near relation, one deeply interested in the queen of clubs, is represented by the queen of diamonds. The ace of clubs shows that a letter is on its way.

The nine of hearts, the wish or betrothal card, follows, and from this I should infer that a proposal of marriage will come by letter, and one which will most probably be accepted. The knave of spades is followed by the seven of diamonds and the eight of hearts, which shows that the queen of clubs has been much loved by someone, and that an offer of marriage will have to be considered either directly before or immediately after a journey. The inquirer will have a great deal of pleasure on a journey. The queen of hearts and knave of diamonds indicate good friends who show her much kindness, and there will be welcome tidings for her across the water.

Now count the rows and should the betrothal card (the nine of hearts) appear in the third or fourth row, that number of years must elapse before becoming engaged.

Count the rows again until the one in which the ten of hearts (the marriage card) appears. In this example the betrothal and marriage card both appear in the third row, which indicates that the inquirer will be engaged in about three years, and marriage will take place soon after.

THE FRENCH METHOD

FRENCH SYSTEM

Take the pack of thirty-two cards, shuffle them thoroughly, then cut them in the usual way and deal them out in two packs of sixteen cards each. The inquirer must choose one of the packs and the first card is placed apart, facedown, to supply the surprise. The remaining fifteen cards must then be turned face upwards, and placed in order from left to right before the dealer. It is essential that the card representing the inquirer should be in the pack selected by him or her, otherwise it is useless to proceed; the cards must be shuffled, cut and dealt out over and over again until the representative card is found in the chosen pack.

THE READING

The reading is conducted as follows. First take any two, three, or four of a kind–kings, knaves, eights, or whatever may appear—and give their explanation as pairs, triplets, or quartets; then start from the representative card and count in sevens from right to left, finally, pair the end cards together and consider their meaning. The next move is to shuffle the fifteen cards again, cut and deal them out into three packs, each of which will naturally have five cards. The first card of the three packs is removed and placed with that card, which has been set apart for "The Surprise," and this way there will be four packs containing an equal number of cards (4 in each pack).

The inquirer must then be asked to choose one of these packs for himself or herself, after which the four cards are exposed on the table from left to right, and their individual and collective meanings are read. The left-hand pack will be for "The House," the third pack is "For Those Who Do Not Expect It," and the fourth "The Surprise."

AN EXAMPLE

Here is an example of the way in which the packs may turn out. We will suppose that the inquirer is represented by the queen of clubs. Her choice falls on the middle pack which contains the following cards: the knave of clubs, the eight of diamonds, reversed, the eight of hearts and the queen of spades.

1. FOR THE INQUIRER

Knave of Clubs	★ Eight of Diamonds ★	Eight of Hearts	Queen of Spades

The reading will be thus, taking the cards in the above order: The thoughts of the inquirer are running upon an unsuccessful love affair, and though moving in a good society, she is exposed to the interference of a dark, malicious widow.

The next pack, standing for "The House," is made up of the knave of spades, the ace of spades, the king of spades, and the knave of hearts. We will take their significations as they stand. The three spades mean disappointment. The presence of two knaves together speaks of evil intentions. The legal agent, knave of spades, is employed in some underhand business by his master, king of spades, the dishonest lawyer, who is an enemy to the inquirer as he is to her friend, the festive, thoughtless young bachelor, knave of hearts, who follows him.

2. THE HOUSE

Knave of Spades	Ace of Spades	King of Spades	Knave of Hearts

The third pack is composed of the nine of clubs, reversed, the ace of clubs, the ten of spades, and the queen of hearts. We find short-lived joy and good news, followed by tears for the fair, soft-hearted lady, who is susceptible to the attractions of the other sex.

3. FOR THOSE WHO DO NOT EXPECT

★ Nine of Clubs ★	Ace of Clubs	Ten of Spades	Queen of Hearts

"The Surprise" is very closely connected with the inquirer herself, for we find her included in the four cards. These are the ace of hearts, the queen of clubs, the nine of diamonds, and the seven of diamonds. From this we gather that there is a love letter for the inquirer, which, however, may be delayed by some accident, and she will be exposed to the foolish ridicule of tactless, unkind persons. But she will get the letter all the same.

4. THE SURPRISE

Ace of Hearts	Queen of Clubs	Nine of Diamonds	Seven of Diamonds

THE GRAND STAR METHOD

The number of cards may vary—The method—the reading in pairs—Diagram of the Grand Star—An example.

THE NUMBER OF CARDS MAY VARY

There are various ways of telling fortunes with cards arranged in the form of a star, and whichever of these may be preferred, it will always be found necessary to use an uneven number of cards in addition to the one representing the inquirer. Some stars are done with thirteen cards, some with fifteen, and so on, but the real Grand Star must have twenty-one cards placed round the representative one.

THE METHOD

Supose the inquirer be a fair man, the king of hearts would be the card selected to form the center of the star. This representative card is placed face upwards on the table, and the remaining thirty-one cards of the pack (the twos, threes, fours, fives, and sixes having been previously removed) must then be shuffled, and cut with the left hand.

The cards are numbered in the order that the are placed in upon the table, taking the representative as

No. 1. The mode of withdrawing the cards from the pack is as follows: The first ten cards are thrown aside after the first cut, and the eleventh card is placed below No. 1; then cut a second time, and place the top card of the pack on the table above No. 1; cut a third time, take the bottom card of the pack and place it to the left of No. 1. The cards must be cut every time a card is to be withdrawn, and they are taken alternately from the top and bottom of the pack. Great care should be observed in the placing of the cards in proper order, as any deviation will affect the reading at a subsequent stage of the process. The last card, No. 22, is placed across the foot of the representative.

THE READING IN PAIRS

When the Grand Star has been formed, the cards must read in pairs, taking the outside circle in this order: 14 and 16, 21 and 19, 15 and 17, 20 and 18. Then take the inner circle, moving from left to right thus: 6 and 10, 9 and 12, 8 and 13, 7 and 11; the four center points are paired thus: 4 and 2, 5 and 3; and the last card, No. 22, is taken separately. The significations are of course taken with regard to the relative positions of the cards, and their special reference to the central figure of the inquirer. This is a picturesque and simple way of consulting the cards, and will probably be a favorite with most people.

AN EXAMPLE

We will take the king of hearts as representative of the inquirer; the twenty-one cards come out in the following order:—

    1. King of hearts

2. Ten of spades
3. Ten of hearts
4. Ace of hearts
5. Nine of spades
6. Ace of spades
7. Nine of diamonds, reversed
8. Queen of hearts
9. Knave of diamonds
10. Queen of spades
11. Knave of clubs
12. King of clubs
13. Eight of clubs
14. Queen of diamonds
15. Nine of clubs, reversed
16. King of spades
17. Queen of clubs
18. Eight of diamonds, reversed
19. Ace of diamonds
20. Knave of spades
21. Knave of hearts
22. Ace of clubs

Before taking these in pairs as directed, it will be well to glance at the groups contained in the star as it lies before us. We find:—

Four aces—Love troubles and hasty news for the inquirer.

Three kings—Success in an important undertaking.

Four queens—A good deal of social intercourse.

Four knaves—Somewhat noisy conviviality.

Two tens—Unexpected good luck.

Three nines—Health, wealth, and happiness, discounted by imprudence since one is reversed.

Two eights—Passing love fancies, one being reversed.

The king of hearts, a fair, open-handed, good-natured man is the starting point in reading the pairs which surround him. He is connected with (14) the queen of diamonds, a fair woman with a tendency to flirtation. She is amusing herself with (16) a very dark man, probably a lawyer, of an ambitious and not too scrupulous character, who does not wish well to the inquirer. The next pair (21) shows the knave of hearts representing Cupid or the thoughts of the one concerned, linked with (19) the ace of diamonds, a wedding ring. While this important item is occupying his thoughts he gives a small present (15), the nine of clubs, reversed, to (17) the queen of clubs, a charming dark lady who is the real object of his affections. (20) The knave of spades, representing a legal agent or the wily lawyer's thoughts, makes mischief, and (18) the eight of diamonds, reversed, causes inquirer's love making to be unsuccessful. (6) The ace of spades warns the inquirer against false friends who will frustrate his matrimonial projects, and in (10) we find one of them, the queen of spades, a widow with possible designs upon him herself; (9) the knave of diamonds, reversed, shows the mischief-maker trying to breed strife with the inquirer's trusty friend (12), the king of clubs, and (8) the queen of hearts, a fair, lovable woman possessing (13) eight of clubs, a dark person's affections; (7) the nine of diamonds, reversed, tells of a love quarrel, owing to (11) the knave of clubs, reversed, a harmless flirt. The inquirer will get (4) the ace of hearts, a love letter, but his happiness will be succeeded by (2) the ten of spades, a card of bad import; (5) the nine of spades tells of grief or sickness, possibly news of a death; but (3) the ten of hearts counteracts the evil, and promises happiness to the inquirer, who will triumph over the obstacles in his path, and find (22) joy in love and life.

IMPORTANT QUESTIONS

When an answer to an important question is required, and the inquirer wishes to consult the cards on the subject, the following simple method may be adopted.

Let the question be asked by the inquirer, then let the dealer take the pack of thirty-two cards, which must be shuffled and cut in the usual manner. The dealer throws out the first eleven cards, which are not used, and proceeds to turn up the others upon the table. The answer is determined by the absence or presence of the special cards applying to each question among the exposed twenty-one.

SPECIMEN QUESTIONS

We will give some examples. Supposing the question to be:—

"How far off is the wedding?"

The needful cards in this case are the queen of spades, who should come out with or near the queen of hearts, and the ace of spades, which should accompany the eight of diamonds. These must be taken in conjunction with the other eights—each of which signifies a year; the four nines—each of which stands for a month; and the four sevens—each of which represents a week. Supposing the above-named cards—the two queens, the ace of spades, and the eight of diamonds—

should not come out in due order, or be absent altogether, it may be feared that the date is postponed to
vanishing point.

"Have I real cause for jealousy?"

If the seven of diamonds comes out in the first fifteen cards, the answer is "Yes." If the five of hearts and
the seven of clubs appear instead among the first fifteen,
it means "No."

"Shall we be parted?" or "Shall I sustain the loss of
my goods?"

If the four nines are included in the twenty-one
cards, the answer is "Yes." Should the four kings and
the four queens come out, the meaning is "No, never!"

"Shall I succeed in my present or projected undertaking?"

To insure a favorable answer the four aces and the
nine of hearts must come out. Should the nine of spades
appear just before the card representing the inquirer, it
foretells failure, sure and certain.

"Will the change of residence or condition that I am
considering be satisfactory?"

Should the question be asked by the master or mis-
tress of a house, or an employer of labor, a favorable
answer is obtained by the presence of the four knaves,
the eight and ten of diamonds, and the ten of clubs.
In the event of the inquirer being an employee, or a
paid worker of any grade, the twenty-one cards must

include the ten and seven of diamonds, the eight of spades, and the four queens, to insure a satisfactory reply. In both cases the nine of diamonds means hindrances and delay in attaining success.

"What fortune does the future hold for this child?"

The four aces foretell good luck and a suitable marriage. If the child in question is a girl, the four eights and the king of hearts should come out to secure peace and concord for her in the home of her husband.

CUPID AND VENUS AT WORK

Among the many ways in which cards can be used to provide entertainment, seasoned with a spice of the unexplainable, the following round game may be given a prominent place:—

The ace of diamonds is the most valuable asset in winning tricks, as it takes all the other cards.
The pack of fifty-two cards is used.
The queen of hearts represents Venus.
The knave of hearts stands for Cupid.
The knave of clubs represents a sweetheart.
The knave of diamonds represents a sweetheart.
The knave of spades represents a sweetheart.
The ace of hearts—a new house.
The ace of clubs—conquest.
The two of diamonds—the ring and marriage.
The twos of clubs, spades and hearts—good luck.
The threes—show surprise.
The fours—present conditions will remain unchanged.
The fives—lovers' meetings.

The sixes—pleasure.

The eights—mirth.

The nines—change.

The tens—marriage settlements.

The queens represent women.

The kings represent men.

Any number may take part in the game. The dealer is chosen by lot, and when this has been settled, he or she proceeds to deal out the cards, leaving ten face downwards on the table. The stakes are agreed upon, and each player puts into the pool, the dealer being expected to pay double for the honor done to him by the fates.

The cards are then taken up, and each player looks at his own hand. The dealer calls for the queen of hearts, Venus, who ranks next to the ace of diamonds in value. Should any one have the ace of diamonds in his hand, he plays it straight out. Should the ace not be among those that have been dealt, the queen of hearts is supreme and the happy holder of Venus may look confidently forward to standing before the altar of Hymen during the current year. If the ace of diamonds player holds both Cupid and Venus in his hand, he wins the pool, and so ends the game right off. In the event that the holder of these cards is married, their presence promises him some special stroke of good fortune.

When the matrimonial cards are out, or proved absent, the game is played on similar lines to whist, the same order of precedence being observed in taking tricks, and the larger the number taken the better the luck of the winner during the current year.

The nine of spades is the worst card in the pack, and the unfortunate holder has to pay for its presence in his hand by a triple stake to the pool. Should any player fail to win any tricks, he must pay in advance the stakes agreed upon for the next game.

MARRIAGE BY LOT SYSTEM

For this appeal to the fates we require a pack of cards, a bag, and stakes either in money or counters. When the players have fixed upon their stakes and placed them in the pool, one of those playing must thoroughly shuffle the pack of cards and place them in the bag. The players then stand in a circle and draw three cards in turn from the bag as it is handed to each of them. Pairs of any kind win back the stakes paid by the holder and promise good luck in the immediate future. The knave of hearts is proclaimed to represent Hymen. He wins double stakes, and is a happy augury that the holder will soon be united to the partner of his or her choice. Should Venus, the queen of hearts, be found in the same hand, the owner takes the pool and wins the game. Fours and eights are losses and crosses, compelling a prearranged payment to the pool in addition to the usual stakes. A lady who draws three nines may resign herself to a life of single-blessedness, and the one who has three fives must prepare to cope with a bad husband.

YOUR FATE IN TWENTY CARDS METHOD

Only three or four girls are required to pursue this search for hidden knowledge. All the kings, queens, knaves, aces and threes must be taken from the pack and dealt round to the players. Each one examines her hand for an answer to her inward questionings. The one who holds the most kings possesses the largest number of friends. The one with the most queens has a proportionate number of enemies. Where kings and

queens are united, there is a promise of speedy and
happy marriage. Should a queen come out with knaves,
we may be sure that intrigues are being woven round
some unlucky person. Knaves by themselves represent
lovers. Threes are evil omens betokening great sorrow.
A knave with four threes means that the fair holder will
not enter the holy estate. A king with four threes en-
courages her to hope, for she has a good chance of
matrimony. A queen with four threes is the worst
combination a girl can draw, for it speaks of sorrow
deepened by disgrace. Mixed hands have no special
significance, nor is there any great meaning attached
to the four aces. Where only two or three of one kind
of card fall together, the meaning ascribed to the four
collectively is lessened in proportion to the number
held.

HEARTS ARE TRUMPS GAME

This game might be called by some an apology for
whist. Four players, or three and a dummy, are necessary, and the whole pack is dealt out in the usual
way. Hearts are trumps in every deal, and carry
everything before them. The highest card is the queen,
who is the goddess of love, and takes precedence to the
ace, which only counts as one. The person on the left
hand of the dealer leads trumps, and the stronger the
hand the better the chances for love and marriage. The
one who wins the largest number of tricks has, or will
have, the most lovers. The presence of the king and
queen of trumps in one hand is the sign of a speedy
union of hearts, and of the approaching sound of wedding bells. A sorry fate awaits the luckless maid or
youth who is without a heart—in the hand—for Cupid
and Hymen have turned their faces away, and no luck
will come of a love affair in that quarter. Where only

one or two small trumps can be produced, the holder will have to wait long for wedded bliss. Each one plays quite independently of the others, and the one who acts as dummy must not connect its cards in any way with those he holds himself.

ANOTHER LOTTERY METHOD

Put a well-shuffled pack of cards into a bag deep enough to prevent the contents from being seen. An uneven number of girls must then form a ring around the one holding the bag, and each must draw a card. The cards drawn must then all be exposed as they have to be compared. The lucky lady who draws the highest card will be the first to be led to the altar. She who draws the lowest will have to resign herself to the fact that "he cometh not" for many weary days to follow. Any one drawing the ace of spades may cheerfully prepare for the pleasures of a bachelor life. The nine of hearts is an omen of serious trouble coming to the holder through loving "not wisely but too well."

ITALIAN METHOD

Only thirty-two cards are used for the Italian method of fortune-telling, all the numbers under seven, except the ace, being taken out of each suit. This reduced pack—containing the ace, king, queen, knave, ten, nine, eight, and seven of the four suits—must be carefully shuffled and cut, with the left hand of course, by the inquirer. The one who is going to act as interpreter then takes the pack and turns them up three at a time. Should three cards of one suit be turned up at once, they are all laid upon the table face upwards; if only two of a suit come out together, the higher card is selected; if all three belong to different suits, they are all rejected.

When the pack has been dealt out in this manner, the cards that have not been chosen are taken up, shuffled and cut a second time. The deal by threes is then repeated until there are fifteen cards upon the table. They must be placed in line from left to right as they appear.

It is absolutely necessary that the card representing the inquirer should be among those on the table. Some authorities maintain that in the event of its not showing up during the deals, the whole process must be repeated until it makes its appearance. Others simply take the card out of the deck and place it on the table when fourteen others have been selected.

The next step is to count five cards from the representative one, and to continue counting in fifths from each fifth card until all have been included, or the counting has come back to the representative. The signification of every card is read as it is reached, notice being taken as to whether it is reversed or not. The surrounding circumstances must also be balanced by the interpreter.

When this reading is complete, the fifteen cards must be paired, one from each end of the line being taken and read together, while the remaining odd one must be dealt with separately.

The third process is to shuffle and cut the fifteen cards and deal them out into five small packs: one for the lady herself; one for the house; one for those who do not expect it; one for the surprise; and one, which is not to be covered, for consolation. When the fifteen cards have been dealt out it will be seen that four of the packs contain three cards, and the fifth only two. These must all be turned face upwards and read in separate packs, but with the connecting idea that they all refer to the fortune of the inquirer.

AN EXAMPLE

Let us imagine that a very fair lady, represented by the queen of diamonds, is seeking to read her fortune.

The fifteen cards come out in the following order:—

The queen of diamonds; nine of diamonds, reversed; queen of hearts; king of spades; ten of diamonds; seven of diamonds, reversed; knave of hearts, reversed; ten of hearts; knave of diamonds; ace of diamonds, reversed; knave of spades; nine of spades; king of clubs; ten of spades, reversed; ace of hearts.

We begin to count from the queen of diamonds, the representative card, and find the nine of diamonds to be the fifth from it. By this first count we see from the nine being reversed that there is a love quarrel troubling the inquirer. Starting again from the nine we come to the queen of hearts, a mild, good-natured, but not very wise woman, who is probably the tool of the next fifth card, the king of spades, a crafty, ambitious man, and an enemy to the queen of diamonds.

Our next count is to the ten of diamonds, which speaks of a journey for the inquirer. Passing on the seven of diamonds, reversed, we get hold of a foolish scandal connected with, if not entirely caused by the next count, which is the knave of hearts, reversed, and stands for a military man who is very discontented with the treatment he has received at the hands of the fair inquirer. She will, however, triumph over this foolish annoyance, for the ten of hearts comes next in order and counteracts the harm involved by the other cards.

Our gentle lady has, unfortunately, an unfaithful friend in the knave of diamonds, reversed, which portends a letter on the way, containing bad news. The writer of this is a dark young man of no social position, and he probably is the servant of one who is dear to the queen of diamonds. The bad news is found in the next count, the nine of spades, which tells of sickness affecting the king of clubs, the warm-hearted, chivalrous man who occupies first place in the inquirer's affections. The last count but one brings us to the ten of spades, reversed, by which we know that the lady's sorrow will be but brief; and it is followed by the ace of hearts, a love letter containing the good news of her lover's recovery.

NOTICE THE GROUPS

Before proceeding to pair the cards, we may as well note the groups as they have come out in the fifteen. The six diamonds point to there being plenty of money; the two tens tell of a change of residence either brought about by marriage or by the journey read in the ten of diamonds; the presence of three knaves betokens false friends, though as one is reversed their power of doing harm is lessened; two queens indicate gossip and the revealing of secrets; the two aces imply an attempted plot but it is frustrated by the one being reversed; the two nines also point to riches.

HOW THE PAIRS WORK OUT

The two end cards of the fifteen are taken up together, so that the pairs shall work out thus:

The queen of diamonds and the nine of spades, implying that sickness and trouble will affect the inquirer; the ten of diamonds pairs with the ten of hearts and they signify a wedding; the knaves of diamonds and spades coming together show evil intentions towards the inquirer; the king of clubs and the ace of hearts tell of the lover and the love letter; the inverted nine of diamonds pairing with the knave of spades tells of a love quarrel, in which a dark young man, wanting in refinement, is concerned; the reversed seven of diamonds pairs with the knave of hearts, also inverted, and tells of a foolish scandal instigated by the ungallant soldier who is suffering from wounded vanity; the inverted ace of diamonds comes out with the queen of hearts, telling of a letter containing unpleasant news from a fair, good-natured woman; while the remaining card, the ten of spades, being inverted, speaks of brief sorrow for the inquirer.

THE FIVE PACKS

Our next step is to deal out the five packs as already directed. The first one—for the lady herself—contains three cards, two of which are bad, but their harm is largely discounted by the ten of hearts. In the nine of spades we read of the trouble caused by her lover's illness; the ten of spades betokens the tears she will shed while the beloved's life is in danger; the ten of hearts speaks of happiness triumphing over sorrow.

The second pack—for the house—contains a flush of diamonds, the ten, the ace, and the knave. There is plenty of money in the house; the ten speaks of a journey, possibly resulting in a change of residence; the ace, being reversed, tells of a letter on the way containing unpleasant news, probably connected with the removal of the knave, who is a faithless friend and is to blame for the annoyance.

The third pack—for those who do not expect—consists of three court cards which taken together foretell gaiety of some sort. We find the inquirer, personified by the queen of diamonds, in the society of the knaves of spades and hearts, the latter reversed, and conse-

quently we know that she will be troubled by some un-
friendly schemes, in which the dark, undesirable young
man and the disappointed officer will be concerned.
The inversion of the one knave counteracts the intended harm.

The fourth pack—for those who do expect—contains
the queen of hearts, the king of spades, and the seven
of diamonds, inverted. These indicate that the fair
woman of gentle and affectionate nature will be exposed to scandal, seven of diamonds reversed; through
the agency of the king of spades, an ambitious, untrust-
worthy lawyer, who is her enemy.

The fifth pack, consisting of only two cards (the ace
of hearts and the nine of diamonds) is for the surprise,
and we learn that a love letter, the ace, will be delayed,
the nine; but the consolation card is the king of clubs,
the dark, warm-hearted man, who will come in person
to his lady-love.

The above example has been given in the plainest,
most straightforward manner with just the most appar-
ent reading of the cards, given as an illustration of the
method. Those who spend time and thought on the
subject will soon get to see more of the "true inward-
ness" of the cards with respect to their relative positions, and their influence one upon another. Various
experiments with this method of fortune-telling will
give rise to curious combinations and perhaps startling
developments, as the one interpreting for the inquirer
gains in knowledge and confidence.

THE PROFESSIONAL METHOD

KNOWLEDGE IS POWER

We have here a detailed and exhaustive method by which the cards can be read. The beginner may feel somewhat alarmed at the mass of explanatory matter there is for him to study, but when once the information has been acquired, the would-be cartomancer will find he possesses a sense of power and comprehension, that will give both confidence and dexterity to his attempts to unravel the thread of destiny.

FOUR TWOS ARE ADDED TO
THE USUAL PACK

The selected pack of thirty-two cards, which have been mentioned in connection with several of the preceding methods, are in this case augmented by the addition of the four twos, one of which is sometimes taken as the representative of the inquirer. There is no hard and fast rule about this, however, and another card may be taken if preferred. The accompanying table shows that not only has each card its own signification, but that every position upon the table within the cube in which the cards are arranged has its own meaning. These must be carefully studied, first separately and then together. It would be a help to the beginner to make a separate chart for his own use, and to have it at hand when laying the cards according to this system.

The thirty-six cards must be shuffled and cut in the usual way, and then placed upon the table in six rows of six cards each, starting from the left-hand corner, where square No. 1 is marked on the chart. The position of the inquirer must be carefully noted, and then all the cards in his immediate neighborhood must be read in all their individual bearing, with regard to their position, and their influence upon the representative card.

THE THIRTY-SIX SQUARES AND THEIR SIGNIFICANCE

We will take the meanings of the thirty-six squares in connection with the several cards that may cover them.

NO. 1—THE PROJECT IN HAND

When covered by a heart, the inquirer may hope that the project will be successfully carried out.

When covered by a club, kind and trusty friends will help forward the project.

When covered by a diamond, there are serious business complications in the way of the project's accomplishment.

When covered by a spade, the inquirer will have his trust abused and those in whom he has confided will play him false to the detriment of the project in hand.

NO. 2—SATISFACTION

When covered by a heart, the inquirer may look for the realization of his brightest hopes and his dearest wishes.

TABLE OF THE POSITIONS AND THEIR MEANINGS

No. 1 Project in hand.	No. 2 Satisfaction.	No. 3 Success.	No. 4 Hope.
No. 5 Chance. Luck.	No. 6 Wishes. Desire.	No. 7 Injustice.	No. 8 Ingratitude.
No. 9 Association.	No. 10 Loss.	No. 11 Trouble.	No. 12 State or Condition.
No. 13 Joy.	No. 14 Love.	No. 15 Prosperity.	No. 16 Marriage.
No. 17 Sorrow. Affliction.	No. 18 Pleasure. Enjoyment.	No. 19 Inheritance. Property.	No. 20 Fraud. Deceit.
No. 21 Rivals.	No. 22 A Present. Gift.	No. 23 Lover.	No. 24 Advancement. A Rise In The World.
No. 25 Kindness. A Good Turn.	No. 26 Undertaking. Enterprise.	No. 27 Changes.	No. 28 The End. (of Life)
No. 29 Rewards.	No. 30 Misfortune. Disgrace.	No. 31 Happiness.	No. 32 Money. Fortune.
No. 33 Indifference.	No. 34 Favor.	No. 35 Ambition.	No. 36 Ill-health. Sickness.

When covered by a club, satisfaction will be derived by the help of true friends who will do all in their power to promote the inquirer's happiness.

When covered by a diamond, there will be jealousy at work to mar the inquirer's satisfaction.

When covered by a spade, the hope of success will be well-nigh shattered by deceit and double-dealing.

NO. 3—SUCCESS

When covered by a heart, the inquirer may hope for complete success.

When covered by a club, any success will be due to the help of friends.

When covered by a spade, all chance of success will be eventually destroyed by underhand means.

NO. 4—HOPE

When covered by a heart, the inquirer may look for the fulfillment of his dearest hopes.

Covered by a club, hopes will be realized through the agency of helpful friends, or be due to the obstinate determination of the inquirer.

Covered by a diamond, it shows that the hopes are groundless and impossible of realization.

Covered by a spade, wild hopes are indicated, tending to mania, and provocative of grave trouble, or even tragedy.

NO. 5—CHANCE—LUCK

Covered by a heart, good luck will attend the hopes and plans of the inquirer.

Covered by a club, means moderately good luck, especially due to the kindly offices of friends.

Covered by a diamond, does not promise much luck to the inquirer; rather an evil than a good influence.

Covered by a spade, bad luck, robbery, financial ruin, disaster and possibly death.

NO. 6—WISHES—DESIRES

Covered by a heart and surrounded by good cards, it promises the immediate fulfillment of the inquirer's highest desires.

Covered by a club, a partial gratification of the inquirer's wishes may be expected.

Covered by a diamond, the earnest efforts of both the inquirer and his friends will only be crowned with imperfect success.

Covered by a spade, disappointment and nonfulfillment of desires.

NO. 7—INJUSTICE

Covered by a heart, any injustice done to the inquirer will be rectified and removed, so that the passing cloud will turn to his ultimate advantage.

Covered by a club, the wrong already done will require long and courageous efforts to wipe out its effects, and the inquirer will need the support of his best friends.

Covered by a diamond, the harm done will not be entirely remedied, but the inquirer's good name will be reestablished.

Covered by a spade, injustice will bring about sore trouble and serious misfortunes.

NO. 8—INGRATITUDE

The four suits have exactly the same influence upon the situation in this number as in the preceding one.

NO. 9—ASSOCIATION

Covered by a heart, the partnership will be successful and have the best results.

Covered by a club, good results of co-operation or partnership will be effected through the agency of true friends.

Covered by a diamond, the inquirer will need to use all possible caution and diplomacy, and even then the results will be unsatisfying.

Covered by a spade, the connection will not benefit the inquirer, in fact he may suffer terribly from it but his friends will profit thereby.

NO. 10—LOSS

Covered by a heart, shows loss of a benefactor, which will be a great grief to the inquirer.

Covered by a club, the loss of dear friends and the failure of cherished hopes.

Covered by a diamond, loss of money, goods, property and personal effects.

Covered by a spade, the best interests of the inquirer will be seriously compromised, and he will have to renounce them.

NO. 11—TROUBLE

Covered by a heart, very great trouble caused by near relations, or born of love for another.

Covered by a club, trouble with friends.

Covered by a diamond, money troubles.

Covered by a spade, trouble arising from jealousy.

NO. 12—STATE OR CONDITION

Covered by a heart, the conditions of life are steadily improving.

Covered by a club, the improvement will be slower and more uncertain; hard work and good friends are essential to ensure advancement.

Covered by a diamond, the inquirer will only attain a satisfactory position in life after he has overcome numerous and powerful enemies. He will never get very far however.

Covered by a spade, the inquirer's circumstances are bound to go from bad to worse in spite of all he may do.

NO. 13—JOY—DELIGHT

Covered by a heart, deep, unruffled delight, joy of a pure and disinterested nature.

Covered by a club, joy from material causes, better luck or greater prosperity.

Covered by a diamond, joy springing from success in profession or business, gained in spite of jealous opposition.

Covered by a spade, joy from having been able to render a service to a superior, who will not forget it.

NO. 14—LOVE

Covered by a heart, the inquirer will be blessed and happy in his love.

Covered by a club, he may rely absolutely upon the fidelity of his beloved.

Covered by a diamond, love will be troubled by jealousy.

Covered by a spade, love will be slighted and betrayed.

NO. 15—PROSPERITY

Covered by a heart, the inquirer will enjoy complete and well-merited prosperity.

Covered by a club, foretells moderate prosperity, due to hard work and the kindly offices of friends.

Covered by a diamond, prosperity will be damaged by the jealousy of others.

Covered by a spade, serious misfortunes will arise

in business, brought about by the malice and fraud of other people.

NO. 16—MARRIAGE

Covered by a heart, the inquirer may look forward to a happy marriage.

Covered by a club, foretells a marriage prompted by practical or financial considerations alone.

Covered by a diamond, the married life will be troubled by the jealousy of one or both partners.

Covered by a spade, inquirer will lose the chance of a wealthy marriage through the deceit and jealousy of his enemies.

NO. 17—SORROW—AFFLICTION

Covered by a heart, the inquirer will pass through a love trouble but it will only be of short duration.

Covered by a club, trouble will arise from a quarrel with a dear friend but it will end in complete reconciliation.

Covered by a diamond, there will be sorrow caused by jealousy.

Covered by a spade, bad faith and underhand dealings will bring affliction upon the inquirer.

NO. 18—PLEASURE—ENJOYMENT

Covered by a heart, the inquirer will enjoy the bliss of mutual love, undimmed by even passing clouds.

Covered by a club, there will be love of a more imperfect and superficial character.

Covered by a diamond, love will be tormented and distracted by jealousy.

Covered by a spade, love will be unreal and fleeting, unable to bear the test of time or survive the first disagreement.

NO. 19—INHERITED MONEY OR PROPERTY

Covered by a heart, the inquirer will come into a large inheritance to which he has a legitimate and undisputed right.

Covered by a club, a friend will bequeath a portion of his property or money to the inquirer.

Covered by a diamond, the inquirer will lose part of his rights owing to the jealousy of another person.

Covered by a spade, an entire estate will be stolen from the inquirer by intriguing rivals.

NO. 20—FRAUD—DECEIT

Covered by a heart, the deceiver will be caught in the trap he has laid for the inquirer.

Covered by a club, by the aid of true friends the inquirer will escape from the effects of an act of treachery.

Covered by a diamond, the inquirer will have to suffer great pain from the consequences of deceit, but it will only be a passing trouble.

Covered by a spade, deceit and underhand dealings will culminate in slander which will cost the inquirer many friends and have serious consequences for him.

NO. 21—RIVALS

Covered by a heart, the inquirer will obtain his desire in spite of powerful or puny rivals.

Covered by a club, rivals will be overcome with difficulty, and with the help of generous friends.

Covered by a diamond, a rival will so far outwit the inquirer as to obtain some of the advantage, wealth, or favor for which he is striving.

Covered by a spade, the rival will triumph over the inquirer, robbing him and plunging him into disgrace both with his benefactors and with members of his own immediate circle.

NO. 22—A PRESENT OR GIFT

Covered by a heart, the inquirer will have a very handsome and unexpected present.

Covered by a club, the inquirer will receive a gift that is bestowed upon him from motives of self-interest or in a spirit of vulgar display.

Covered by a diamond, points to a gift intended to act as a bribe.

Covered by a spade, indicates a present which is given to further the deceitful ends of the donor.

NO. 23—LOVER

Covered by a heart, the lover or the lady, as the case may be, will be both fond and faithful in life and death.

Covered by a club, the beloved will be faithful but somewhat faulty in other respects.

Covered by a diamond, the inquirer may be prepared to find the beloved both jealous and disposed to sulk.

Covered by a spade, the beloved will prove faithless, selfish and vindictive.

NO. 24—ADVANCEMENT

Covered by a heart, the inquirer will soon see a rapid improvement in his worldly position and it will exceed his wildest hopes.

Covered by a club, there will be a moderate and satisfying advance in the inquirer's circumstances, which will be the result of his own hard work, aided by the sympathy and help of his friends. He will be contented and happy.

Covered by a diamond, advancement will only be obtained after a hard struggle against difficulties, caused by the jealous ill-will of others.

Covered by a spade, the underhand dealings of his enemies will destroy all hopes of a rise in the world.

NO. 25—KINDNESS—GOOD TURN

Covered by a heart, the inquirer will receive a kindness which far exceeds both his expectations and his deserts.

Covered by a club, this good turn will be well deserved, but only obtained by the help of disinterested friends.

Covered by a diamond, the inquirer will only obtain a modicum of kindness, and that after he has surmounted serious obstacles built up by the jealousy and self-seeking of some people concerned in it.

Covered by a spade, the inquirer must prepare for failure in his enterprise owing to the malicious intrigues of his rivals.

NO. 26—UNDERTAKING—ENTERPRISE

Covered by a heart, whatever undertaking the inquirer has in hand will meet with signal success.

Covered by a club, the enterprise will be a financial success owing to the help of friends.

Covered by a diamond, the success of the undertaking will be hindered and decreased by the jealousy and self-seeking of some people concerned in it.

Covered by a spade, the inquirer must prepare for failure in his enterprise, owing to the malicious intrigues of his rivals.

NO. 27—CHANGES

Covered by a heart, the change contemplated by the inquirer is a good one.

Covered by a club, a change for the better will take place in the inquirer's circumstances owing to the good offices of friends.

Covered by a diamond, the inquirer will make an earnest attempt to change his position in life but his efforts will be fruitless.

Covered by a spade, a change, very much for the worse, is to be apprehended. It will be brought about by the malice and double-dealing of those who seek to harm him.

NO. 28—THE END (of Life)

Covered by a heart, by the death of a relation or friend the inquirer will come into a considerable fortune.

Covered by a club, a handsome legacy from a friend may be expected by the inquirer.

Covered by a diamond, one who wishes ill to the inquirer will depart this life.

Covered by a spade, this portends the untimely death of the inquirer's greatest enemy.

NO. 29—REWARD

Covered by a heart, the inquirer will be rewarded out of all proportion to his efforts.

Covered by a club, a due and fitting reward will be meted out to industry and perseverance.

Covered by a diamond, a well-merited reward will be hindered and reduced by the unscrupulous action of others.

Covered by a spade, the inquirer will be done out of his just reward by the double-dealing and dishonesty of certain people.

NO. 30—DISGRACE—MISFORTUNE

Covered by a heart, misfortune will come to the inquirer but it will not do him any permanent harm.

Covered by a club, the inquirer will suffer through the disgrace of a friend.

Covered by a diamond, misfortune will be brought about by jealousy and will indirectly affect the inquirer.

Covered by a spade, dishonesty and double-dealing will cause disgrace from which the inquirer will suffer long and acutely.

NO. 31—HAPPINESS

Covered by a heart, the inquirer will experience unexpected happiness which will be both deep and lasting.

Covered by a club, a stroke of luck will come to the inquirer through the good offices of friends.

Covered by a diamond, the jealousy and ambition of false friends will result in good fortune to the inquirer.

Covered by a spade, the life of the inquirer will be in danger from the malice of his enemies. Their murderous schemes will be happily defeated by the vigilance of his friends.

NO. 32—MONEY—FORTUNE

Covered by a heart, the inquirer will rapidly acquire a large fortune by making a hit in his profession or by a lucky speculation.

Covered by a club, by hard work and sustained effort the inquirer will secure an income and will receive both help and encouragement from his friends.

Covered by a diamond, through misplaced confidence in unworthy friends the inquirer will see his fortune pass into dishonest hands.

Covered by a spade, not only will the inquirer be tricked out of his money by dishonest acquaintances, but he will have to suffer for their misdeeds in his business or profession.

NO. 33—INDIFFERENCE

Covered by a heart, thanks to his indifference and lack of heart the inquirer will lead an unruffled if somewhat joyless life.

Covered by a club, lack of interest and energy will allow the inquirer to let slip things that would give him pleasure.

Covered by a diamond, the inquirer will forfeit the love and regard of valuable friends owing to indifference and utter unresponsiveness.

Covered by a spade, as a result of culpable indifference the inquirer will be robbed and impoverished.

NO. 34—FAVOR

Covered by a heart, the inquirer will enjoy all that love can bestow upon the beloved.

Covered by a club, the inquirer will honestly seek and acquire the favor of influential persons.

Covered by a diamond, the favor of the great will be long and earnestly sought by the inquirer, who will not succeed single-handed.

Covered by a spade, no effort of any kind will admit the inquirer to the favor to which he aspires.

NO. 35—AMBITION

Covered by a heart, the inquirer will shortly arrive at the highest point of his ambition.

Covered by a club, the moderate ambition of the inquirer will be realized.

Covered by a diamond, the lawful ambitions of the inquirer will be partially frustrated, by the ill-will and jealousy of certain acquaintances.

Covered by a spade, the principal ambition of the inquirer will be defeated by underhand transactions, and he will even suffer from the consequences of perfectly justifiable steps which he may take to accomplish his desire.

NO. 36—SICKNESS—ILL-HEALTH

Covered by a heart, the inquirer will suffer from passing ailments that will leave no bad results.

Covered by a club, a rather serious illness may be expected.

Covered by a diamond, an acute attack of a definite disease.

Covered by a spade, a very severe illness that may materially interfere with the inquirer's career or happiness.

TENDENCIES OF THE SUITS

It will be seen in the foregoing definitions that hearts are almost invariably the sign of good luck, love and happiness. Even where the position is indicative of misfortune, the presence of a heart has a mitigating effect upon the evil. Clubs rank next in order of good fortune, and seem specially connected with the precious gift of true friendship. Diamonds seem accompanied by the disquieting elements of jealousy and rivalry, which strew obstacles in the path to success and happiness, while for sheer bad luck and dire disaster the ill-omened suit of spades stands unrivalled.

SIGNIFICATION OF SUITS IN THE PROFESSIONAL METHOD

Court cards—Plain cards—An example of the Master Method.

HEARTS

THE KING OF HEARTS—In this method he represents a married man or a widower. Should the inquirer be a woman, and this card fall upon either of the squares 14, 22, 23, 24, or 32, he then denotes a lover. Should the inquirer be a man, the king falling in the above-named squares signifies a rival.

When this card falls on either of the following numbers, 2, 3, 4, 13, 14, 15, 16, 18, 19, 23, 24, 29, 31, 32, 34, the situation is favorable, and the inquirer will have his wishes granted with respect to the special meaning of the square.

When the king falls on No. 1, 5, 6, 9, 12, 22, 26, 27, or 28, it foretells a satisfactory solution of any matter connected with the subject represented by the squares.

Should he fall upon an unlucky square, namely, No. 7, 8, 10, 11, 17, 20, 21, 30, 33, 35, or 36, he mitigates the evil fortune of the positions.

THE QUEEN OF HEARTS—She signifies a married woman or a widow who desires the happiness of the inquirer and does her best to promote it.

If the inquirer is a man, this card falling on the squares 14, 22, 23, 24, or 32, represents his lady-love. In the event of his being already engaged, his fiancee will possess all the most lovable and desirable qualities.

When the inquirer is a woman, and the queen of hearts falls on either of the above-named squares, it shows that she has a rival to reckon with. Should she be engaged, it indicates that her future husband is both young and well equipped for social and professional success.

When a very elderly person consults the cards, the

above combination foretells a peaceful, contented old age.

To any one interested in agriculture, the same combination promises abundant crops.

THE KNAVE OF HEARTS—This card represents a good-natured, amiable but rather insipid young man, devoid alike of violent passions and exalted aspirations.

When a young girl consults the cards, this knave falling on the squares 14, 22, 23, 24, or 32, may be taken to personify her fiancee.

When the inquirer is a young, unmarried man, the same combination indicates that he will marry the object of his choice after he has surmounted considerable obstacles by his tact and quiet determination.

THE TEN OF HEARTS—The signification of this card does not differ from that given in the general definitions save in the following cases:—

When it falls on square No. 10, it signifies success.

When it falls on square No. 14, it signifies success in love.

When it falls on square No. 16, it signifies a happy marriage.

If in the last-named case, a knave or a seven falls on No. 7, 15, 17, or 25, there will be several children born of the union.

If the ten of hearts falls on squares 18, 19, 31, or 32, it foretells wealth, intense enjoyment, and real happiness.

THE NINE OF HEARTS—The only addition to the general signification is that when this card falls near the seven of clubs, it denotes that a promise already made to the inquirer will shortly be fulfilled.

THE EIGHT OF HEARTS—This card is the special messenger of good things when it falls on one of the following squares: 5, 9, 15, 18, 19, 22, or 31.

THE SEVEN OF HEARTS—If this card falls on No. 14, 22, 23, 24, or 32, when the inquirer is a bachelor, it signifies that he will very soon take unto himself a wife.

THE TWO OF HEARTS—This is frequently taken as the representative card, and in that case is entirely influenced by its position on the chart taken in connection with the cards that touch or surround it.

THE ACE OF HEARTS—This card represents the house of the inquirer as it does in other methods. It is very important to note its position on the chart and its surroundings.

CLUBS

THE KING OF CLUBS—Taken generally, this card represents a married man or a widower whose worth as a friend is not to be excelled.

When the inquirer is a young girl and this king falls on No. 14, 22, 23, 24, or 32, she may rejoice for she will shortly be united in marriage to the man she loves.

Should a young man be consulting the cards, this king falling on any of the above-named squares denotes a generous, high-minded rival who will meet him in fair fight, and who is far above anything like taking a mean advantage.

When this card falls on No. 18, 19, 20, 27 or 28, it

represents the guardian of a minor, whose line of conduct will be determined by the cards which surround or touch it.

THE QUEEN OF CLUBS—When a bachelor consults the cards, and this queen falls on No. 14, 22, 23, 24 or 32, it promises him a lady-love whose beauty shall be her strongest attraction.

Should a woman be seeking to know her fate, this queen falling on either of the above-named squares warns her that she has a rival. In the case of the inquirer being a married man or woman, this card represents a woman of high position and great influence who is attractive to the inquirer, and who will be the means of bringing him or her valuable and pleasing intelligence.

In the case of a businessman the above combination denotes that he will be entirely successful in the enterprise which is engrossing all his thoughts at the moment.

THE KNAVE OF CLUBS—This card may be taken to represent a sincere and lasting friendship founded upon a basis that will endure.

When the inquirer is a young girl and this card falls upon either of the matrimonial squares, namely, 14, 22, 23, 24, or 32, it signifies some man who wants to marry her.

In the case of a bachelor, this card on the same squares tells him that he has a rival, either in love or in his business career.

THE TEN OF CLUBS—This card is the harbinger of good luck if it falls on No. 3, 5, 15, 18, 19, 22, 25, 28, 31, or 32.

Should this card fall on squares 10, 17, or 36, it implies that the inquirer will be asked for a loan of money which he will be unable to lend.

THE NINE OF CLUBS—This card means a present, and if it follows a club, the gift will be in money; if it follows a heart, the inquirer may look for a present of jewelry; if it follows a diamond, the gift will be trifling in value; and if it follows a spade, the recipient of the present will derive no pleasure from it.

THE EIGHT OF CLUBS has no special significance outside the general definition.

THE SEVEN OF CLUBS—This represents a young girl capable of the highest self-devotion, even to risking her life in the interests of the inquirer.

The exact nature of her relations and services to the object of her affection will be decided by the surrounding cards.

In the case of a bachelor, this card falling on any of the squares 14, 22, 23, 24, or 32, represents the lady of his choice.

In the case of an unmarried girl or a widow, the same combination points to a generous rival.

Whenever this seven comes out near the nine of hearts, the wish card, it is a token of some signal success for the inquirer.

THE TWO OF CLUBS—This represents the trusted friend of the inquirer, and the square on which it falls will give the requisite information if its meaning is taken in conjunction with those of the surrounding cards.

THE ACE OF CLUBS—This card is the sign of

a well-ordered life and legitimate hopes, and foretells success in an ordinary career, or the attainment of celebrity in special cases.

Should the inquirer be a soldier, it signifies a fortunate turn of events that will secure him a rapid rise in the army.

To one interested in agriculture, it promises plentiful crops.

To a traveler, it foretells a most satisfactory result from his journey.

To an actress, it promises phenomenal success in a leading role. Should the inquirer or one of his parents be a dramatic or musical author, this card is the omen of theatrical success.

DIAMONDS

THE KING OF DIAMONDS—Should the inquirer be a young girl, she will do well to note whether this card falls on any of the matrimonial squares, 14, 22, 23, 24 or 32, for in that case her present admirer is not to be trusted unless he has cards of good import touching him, or is preceded by either a heart or a club.

THE QUEEN OF DIAMONDS—If this card falls on any of the matrimonial squares, 14, 22, 23, 24, or 32, it signifies to a bachelor that he will be engaged to one whose character is to be read in the surrounding cards. If this queen is preceded by a heart or a club, it promises good luck on the whole; but if by a diamond or a spade, the augury is bad.

Should the inquirer be a young unmarried woman or a widow, this card indicates that she has a rival whose character is revealed by the cards touching it.

THE KNAVE OF DIAMONDS—For an unmarried woman or a widow, this card represents a lover from a foreign country. If it is accompanied by a heart, he has many good points to recommend him; if by a club, he is kind and generous; if by a diamond, he is bad-tempered, exacting, undesirable, and she had better have nothing to do with him.

THE TEN OF DIAMONDS—The general meaning of this card is a journey.

If it fall between two spades, the journey will be long.

If it falls between two hearts, the journey will be short.

If it falls between two clubs, the journey will be successful.

If it falls between two diamonds, the journey will have bad results.

THE NINE OF DIAMONDS—This card signifies news. If preceded by a heart or a club, the news will be good. If preceded by a diamond or a spade, the news will be bad.

THE EIGHT OF DIAMONDS—The card signifies a short journey. If it falls between two hearts, the expedition will be an enjoyable pleasure trip.

If between two clubs, it denotes a satisfactory business journey.

If between two diamonds, it signifies a trip begun for pleasure and ending in misadventure.

If between two spades, it signifies an unsuccessful business journey.

THE SEVEN OF DIAMONDS—This card stands for a young girl of foreign birth and breeding. Taken by itself it means love-sorrows and heart-searchings.

Should the inquirer be a bachelor and this card fall on one of the matrimonial squares, 14, 22, 23, 24, or 32, it signifies a lady-love as above described.

This seven is an excellent augury when it falls on No. 2, 3, 15, 16, 18, or 27.

THE TWO OF DIAMONDS—has practically the same significance as the deuce of clubs, unless it is selected as the representative card.

THE ACE OF DIAMONDS—The significance of this card is a letter.

If preceded by a heart, it is a letter from a lover or friend.

If preceded by a club, it is a letter on business or one containing money.

If preceded by a diamond, the letter is dictated by jealousy.

If preceded by a spade, the letter contains bad news.

SPADES

THE KING OF SPADES—When the inquirer is an unmarried woman or a widow, this card falling on one of the squares, 14, 22, 23, 24, or 32, is indicative of a false lover whose character is mean and base.

When the inquirer is an unmarried man, the above combination signifies that he has a rival.

This card falling on the squares numbered 10, 18, 19, 20, 27, 28, or 29, represents a guardian or the executor of a will.

To a married man, this king is a warning that there are domestic ructions in store for him.

To a married woman, the card cautions her to be

very much on her guard when in the society of an attractive but unprincipled man whom she has to meet frequently, and who will bring scandal upon her if she is not most careful.

THE QUEEN OF SPADES—When the inquirer is a bachelor, this card falling on No. 14, 22, 23, 24, or 32, represents the lady to whom he will be engaged.

In the case of an unmarried woman or a widow, the combination signifies a rival in love.

THE KNAVE OF SPADES, THE TEN OF SPADES, THE NINE OF SPADES, AND THE EIGHT OF SPADES have no special signification other than that given in the general definitions.

THE SEVEN OF SPADES—This card signifies all troubles and worries connected with the tender passion.

Should the inquirer be a man, this seven falling on squares 14, 22, 23, 24, or 32 foretells faithlessness on the part of his fiancee, a betrayal of trust by some other woman or a robbery.

When the inquirer is a woman, this card on any of the same squares points to a rival who will be preferred before her.

THE TWO OF SPADES—may be taken as a representative card but otherwise has no special signification.

THE ACE OF SPADES—is a card of good omen, meaning perseverance followed by possession, a happy marriage, success and rapid advancement in business or profession.

AN EXAMPLE OF THE PROFESSIONAL METHOD

We have taken the deuce of hearts as the representative card of the inquirer, who is a fair young girl seeking to know her fate. We will give the order in which the thirty-six cards come out, but intend to leave the bulk of them for the reader to solve according to the instructions given.

We have taken the inquirer and her immediate surroundings as an example of the working of the method, and feel sure that any intelligent reader will be able to complete the reading for himself.

No. 1 Ace of clubs

No. 2 Eight of spades

No. 3 Two of clubs

No. 4 Knave of hearts

No. 5 King of diamonds

No. 6 King of hearts

No. 7 Eight of diamonds

No. 8 Ten of clubs

No. 9 Ten of hearts

No. 10 Seven of spades

No. 11 Nine of spades

No. 12 Two of spades

No. 13 Nine of hearts

No. 14 Eight of spades

No. 15 Queen of diamonds

No. 16 Two of hearts

No. 17 King of spades

No. 18 Queen of hearts

No. 19 Ace of spades

No. 20 Ten of spades

No. 21 Knave of spades

No. 22 King of clubs

No. 23 Nine of clubs

No. 24 Eight of hearts

No. 25 Queen of clubs

No. 26 Knave of diamonds

No. 27 Queen of spades

No. 28 Seven of diamonds

No. 29 Seven of hearts

No. 30 Ten of diamonds

No. 31 Knave of clubs

No. 32 Ace of diamonds

No. 33 Ace of hearts

No. 34 Seven of clubs

No. 35 Two of diamonds

No. 36 Nine of diamonds

We find the inquirer in No. 16, which square when covered by a heart indicates a happy and well-suited marriage. On her left in No. 15 (prosperity) she has the queen of diamonds, a very fair woman who is fond of gossip, and somewhat wanting in refinement of feeling. She will interfere with the inquirer's prosperity through jealousy, but on the whole she will bring good luck because she is preceded by a club. To the right in No. 17 (sorrow) we have the king of spades, a dark, ambitious, but unscrupulous man who is the in-

quirer's legal adviser and will bring grave sorrow
upon her by his underhand dealings. Immediately
above her we have in No. 10 (loss) the seven of
spades, a card representing troubles connected with a
love affair. This square being covered by a spade indicates that she will be unjustly compelled to relin-
quish her rights and her chance of marriage may be
lessened or postponed by the loss of her fortune.

On the left above her we get in No. 9 (association)
the ten of hearts, a most cheering and excellent card
promising her success and happiness in a partnership
which she is contemplating. On the right, above, in
No. 11 (trouble) we have the nine of spades, a bad
omen signifying the failure of her hopes through the
jealousy of some other person.

Immediately below her we find in No. 22 (a gift)
the king of clubs, who is her true and valued friend,
either a married man or a widower. He will make
her a present and will be actuated by certain motives
of self-interest in so doing; but she may keep a good
heart for his presence in that position on the chart
indicates that she will soon be united to the man of
her choice. On the left, below, in No. 21 (rival) we
find the knave of spades, a legal agent whose influence
will be instrumental in enabling a rival to triumph
over and bring discredit upon the inquirer. On the
right, below, we have in No. 23 (a lover) the nine of
clubs, which in this case means a gift in money. We
may take it that her faithful lover, uninfluenced by
her pecuniary losses, has decided to make her a present probably in the form of a marriage settlement.

The remainder of the chart will provide the student with many more interesting particulars regard-
ing the fate of this fair inquirer, and at the same
time prove an excellent exercise in the art of cartomancy.

No. 1 No. 2 No. 3 No. 4 No. 5 No. 6

	No. 9 Ten of Hearts.	No. 10 Seven of Spades.	No. 11 Nine of Spades.	
No. 7 No. 8	No. 9 Ten of Hearts.	No. 10 Seven of Spades.	No. 11 Nine of Spades.	No. 12
No. 13 No. 14	No. 15 Queen of Diamonds.	No. 16 Inquirer. Deuce of Hearts.	No. 17 King of Spades.	No. 18
No. 19 No. 20	No. 21 Knave of Spades.	No. 22 King of Clubs.	No. 23 Nine of Clubs. Spades.	No. 24

No. 25 No. 26 No. 27 No. 28 No. 29 No. 30
No. 31 No. 32 No. 33 No. 34 No. 35 No. 36

THE WISH WITH 52 CARDS

The fifty-two cards must be shuffled and cut into three packs by the person who wishes to have his or her fortune told, and the fortune-teller must be careful to note what cards appear as the various packs are turned face upwards, as this will assist the reading.

The card representing the inquirer must first be selected.

Then lay the cards nine in a row, beginning from right to left with each row; only seven will be in the last row.

The cards being in order on the table, you must begin by counting nine from your representative card and nine again from the ninth, until you come to a card that has already been counted.

The court cards represent the various people with whom the inquirer is brought into contact, and their relation and attitude are easily determined by the meaning of the cards between. Three deals are necessary for a good reading.

AN EXAMPLE

I give an example of fortune-telling by the combination of nines because an illustration is of practical help.

The pack having been dealt in the manner described, we find the cards have resolved themselves thus, reading from left to right in each row:—

First line—Seven of clubs, seven of spades, king of spades, ace of diamonds, ace of hearts, knave of clubs, four of hearts, eight of hearts, knave cf spades.

Second line—Two of diamonds, three of diamonds, two of hearts, six of hearts, king of diamonds, five of clubs, two of clubs, five of spades, three of hearts.

Third line—Five of hearts, six of diamonds, four of clubs, queen of clubs, five of diamonds, three of spades, king of hearts, four of diamonds, ten of spades.

Fourth line—Nine of spades, queen of spades, eight of diamonds, six of clubs, ace of spades, queen of diamonds, king of clubs, knave of hearts, six of spades, nine of hearts.

Fifth line—Ten of diamonds, eight of clubs, seven of diamonds, ace of clubs, nine of clubs, nine of diamonds, knave of diamonds, ten of hearts, ten of clubs.

Sixth line—Eight of spades, queen of hearts, seven of hearts, four of spades, three of clubs, two of spades.

We will take the queen of hearts to represent the inquirer, and as she is in the lowest line of all, will count upwards. The ninth card is the knave of clubs, and the next ninth the six of hearts, then the three of spades, the ace of spades, and nine of clubs, which brings us back to our queen.

According to the signification given by this method the reading would be as follows:—

Knave of clubs—A generous friend

Six of hearts—Implies credulity

Three of spades—Difficulties. Be careful in making friends

Nine of clubs—Displeasure of friends

THE FIRST READING

My general reading of this would be that if the queen of hearts were an unmarried woman she was in danger of making an unhappy marriage which would bring the displeasure of her friends upon her. If she will avoid forming hasty friendships, and take the advice of a man who is older and darker than herself, she will avoid much misfortune.

If married, the queen is the victim of an ill-matched union, but she must be careful not to give too much credence to the reports of friends and must guard her own conduct carefully.

We will now proceed with the next deal to see if we can find a more favourable augury in the Book of Fate.

THE SECOND READING

First line—Eight of clubs, queen of hearts, six of spades, eight of spades, eight of hearts, six of diamonds, ten of hearts, nine of clubs, six of hearts.

Second line—Three of spades, ace of spades, three of diamonds, king of spades, ace of diamonds, ace of hearts, king of diamonds, king of clubs, ace of clubs.

Third line—Ten of spades, five of clubs, two of hearts, five of hearts, ten of diamonds, four of hearts, two of clubs, knave of spades, three of hearts.

Fourth line—Five of spades, four of clubs, six of clubs, queen of diamonds, four of diamonds, king of hearts, nine of spades, five of diamonds, seven of clubs.

Fifth line—Knave of clubs, ten of clubs, three of clubs, nine of diamonds, queen of spades, seven of spades, knave of hearts, eight of diamonds, seven of diamonds.

Sixth line—Seven of hearts, four of spades, queen of clubs, two of spades, knave of diamonds, two of diamonds, nine of hearts.

Here our inquirer does not prove to be a very wise

person. In spite of the warning and displeasure of friends, regardless of the affection of a good man, and elated through unexpected riches, she listens with credulous mind to one who will cause her much unhappiness. Let us hope she will stop short of one fatal step, and take the good honorable love that is awaiting her.

The ninth card is the king of clubs, and the five of the same suit following in our arranged plan, then the five of diamonds, the ten of clubs, the two of diamonds, the six of hearts, and the three of spades complete this reading. A reference to the signification will show the importance of these cards.

Perhaps in the third reading we may have more success.

THE THIRD READING

First line—Ace of clubs, eight of clubs, queen of hearts, ten of spades, king of clubs, five of diamonds, ten of clubs, nine of spades, knave of spades.

Second line—Three of spades, two of spades, six of hearts, eight of spades, five of spades, knave of clubs, seven of hearts, four of spades, queen of clubs.

Third line—Five of hearts, two of diamonds, three of diamonds, queen of diamonds, eight of hearts, three of clubs, five of clubs, ace of diamonds, six of diamonds.

Fourth line—Four of diamonds, six of clubs, seven of clubs, seven of diamonds, six of spades, nine of diamonds, knave of diamonds, nine of hearts, eight of diamonds.

Fifth line—Ten of hearts, king of spades, two of hearts, ten of diamonds, ace of hearts, four of hearts, king of hearts, king of diamonds, queen of spades.

Sixth line—Two of clubs, seven of spades, knave

of hearts, nine of clubs, three of hearts, four of clubs, ace of spades.

The cards here are more promising, though still full of warning. The ninth card is the seven of hearts which means unfaithfulness, followed by another card indicating domestic dissension. The next is the knave of diamonds and treachery is to be apprehended. But there is considerable success if care is exercised, and later on there appears to be a happy marriage with comfort and even luxury.

Throughout her life the inquirer would have to be on her guard against forming hasty friendships, and refrain from listening to scandal about those near and dear to her. In this care I should think there would be two marriages, the first not happy (which would probably be dissolved by law), then a happier time later in life with one who had been content to wait.

YOUR HEART'S DESIRE SYSTEM

The wish with fifteen cards—Another way—The wish with thirty-two cards—What the four aces tell—The wish in seven packs—The wish card again.

THE WISH WITH FIFTEEN CARDS

Having shuffled the cards well, select according to the second method the card which will represent the inquirer—a king for a man, a queen for a woman—and place this card on the table; then request your subject to wish for some one thing while he or she is shuffling the pack (which must include only the selected thirty-two cards). The pack must be cut once.

Take the cards, and holding them easily in your

own hands, let the inquirer draw fifteen cards placing them face downwards on the table, one on top of the other in the order drawn. The fifteen cards having been drawn, discard the others and place the selected ones in position according to the following plan: The representative card is to be in the center, and the other cards are to be placed to the left—to the right—above—below—and on the center, one by one. Thus on the left you will have the first, sixth, and eleventh; on the right, the second, seventh, and twelfth; above, the third, eighth, and thirteenth; below, the fourth, ninth, and fourteenth; and on the representative card you will have placed the fifth, tenth and fifteenth. (See diagram.)

Then take the left packet and turn and read according to the meaning in the combination of sevens. The next packet to be taken is the one on the right, then the one above, and following that the packet below. The left and top packets represent events that may influence your wish in the future; the packets on the right and below show those events which have influenced it in the past; while those cards covering the representative card indicate affairs that may be expected immediately, and are to be read in strict reference to the wish.

YOUR WISH IN FIFTEEN CARDS

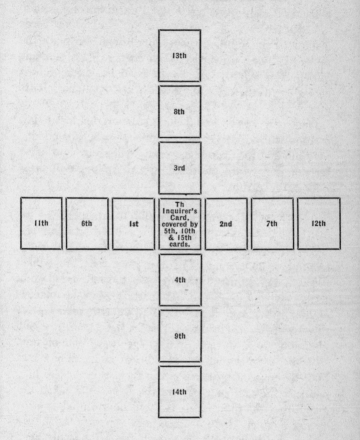

ANOTHER WAY WITH FIFTY-TWO CARDS

Let the inquirer shuffle the cards well, and cut them into three packs, having first selected your representative card as in the former method and placed it in the center of a circle.

Take up the packs and lay the cards in a circle

using forty-two, and with the ramaining nine form a triangle inside the circle. The cards must be laid face down.

Now let the inquirer choose any fifteen cards, which must be faced upwards as he makes his selection. When fifteen cards are chosen, read the signification according to the meaning given in the combination of nines.

Generally speaking, if diamonds predominate the fortune will be fair, if hearts appear in the ascendant, love affairs are prosperous; clubs will show how material interests are progressing; and spades will prepare us for sorrow.

THE WISH WITH THIRTY-TWO CARDS

Take out all the twos, threes, fours, fives, and sixes from an ordinary pack. The inquirer must then shuffle the remaining thirty-two, cut with the left hand, and wish from the depths of his heart. The dealer places eight cards, face downwards, upon the table in a row before him. He next turns them up one by one, beginning from the left, and as soon as a pair of any kind, it does not matter what, be exposed, they must both be covered by cards taken from the pack in his hand. If they all pair off exactly, it may be taken as a sign that the inquirer's wish will be gratified, but if at any moment there are no pairs exposed, the fates are unpropitious, and the search for a favorable answer must be abandoned. Should most of the cards pair off, leaving only one, two or three unmated, it portends delay and disappointment before the realization of the desire.

Take the thirty-two cards up again, shuffle them and mentally register your wish. The first thirteen cards must be turned up and a careful search made for any aces that may be there. If found, place them on one side. The rest of the cards must be shuffled again and thirteen more dealt out, with a second search for aces. This is done a third time if all four have not appeared; and if they still refuse to come there is no hope of the wish being granted. It is the best possible omen if the four aces come out in the first deal, and very good luck if they arrive with only two attempts; but the third is the last chance, so the turning up of those thirteen cards is fraught with much excitement.

THE WISH IN SEVEN PACKS

This is a very simple method, but it is by no means always propitious to the inquirer; if, however, he does get the desired answer we take it that the capricious goddess is in a very smiling mood.

Thirty-two cards are required, and they must be arranged in suits in the following order: Ace, king, queen, knave, ten, nine, eight, seven. The cards must not be shuffled, but the arranged pack is cut with the left hand into seven smaller packs and all are placed face downwards upon the table.

The dealer must then proceed to turn up the top cards of each pack, and as a pair of queens, nines, knaves, or whatever they may happen to be becomes visible, he must remove them from the packs. Should all the cards pair off in this manner, the wish may be taken as one that will speedily be granted. Should the cards come out awkwardly, literally in sixes and sevens instead of pairs, the inquirer must adapt his desires to the inevitable with the best grace he can.

THE WISH CARD AGAIN

Yet a sixth way which will give some idea if the heart's desire will be gratified is as follows:—

Shuffle the whole pack of cards and give them to the inquirer who must then divide the pack into three, wishing intently all the time. Take up the packs separately and glance through them; the nine of hearts is the most important card as that is the symbol of the wish. Should this be in juxtaposition to the card —the king or queen—representing the inquirer and with favorable surroundings, then you may conclude that the things hoped for will come to pass. Also, if the wish card is in combination with cards that are an indication of the inquirer's desires, it is a favorable augury.

For instance, if the wish referred to business, and the suit of clubs surrounded the nine of hearts, then it might be concluded that the matter would terminate in a prosperous manner. Diamonds, as they foretell wealth, would also promise prosperity; hearts imply good wishes and good will, while spades carry a sinister meaning.

A RHYMING DIVINATION

There are those to whom the more elaborate forms of fortune-telling by cards may seem a trifle wearisome, or possibly too intricate to be followed without an exhausting effort of attention. The method which we give in this chapter has the advantage of being at once simple, diverting and varied.

As the rhyming significations concern both sexes a great deal of fun can be provided where there is a party of young people, and who can tell whether the long arm of coincidence may not use this old-time practice to bring some loving pair together?

Take a new pack of cards, or at any rate one in which there are no tell-tale marks on the reverse sides, and spread them face downwards upon the table. Before any one draws a card, he or she is requested to close the eyes, place the right hand on the heart, and say, "Honi soit qui mal y pense." The card must then be drawn with the left hand, and its meaning will be read by the one who holds the key contained in the verses which we now give.

DIAMONDS

Ace—
Since that this ace is now your lot,
You will wed one that's fierce and hot;
But if a woman does draw it,
She will wed one with wealth and wit.

Two—

> Hast thou not drawn the number two?
> Thy spouse shall be both just and true.
> But if a woman this now have,
> Beware a sly and crafty knave!

Three—

> You that have drawn the number three,
> Great honor will your fortune be;
> But if a female draw the same,
> She must beware of fickle shame.

Four—

> The man that draws the number four
> Shall quite forsake his native shore;
> But if the same a woman finds,
> Both hand and heart in love she joins.

Five—

> He that draweth the number five,
> Where he was born he best will thrive;
> But if it's drawn by womankind,
> Good luck abroad they sure will find.

Six—

> He that can catch the number six
> Will have cunning and crafty tricks;
> But if a woman draw the same,
> 'Twill show that she is free from blame.

Seven—

> Since that the seven does appear,
> Crosses thou hast great cause to fear;
> Women, whene'er the same they draw,
> Shall not fear crosses more than straw.

Eight—

Hast thou then drawn the number eight?
Thou sure wilt be a rascal great;
Females that chance the same to take,
They never will the truth forsake.

Nine—

Hast thou turn'd up the merry nine?
Then guineas will thy pocket line;
She that doth draw it to her hand
Will die for love or leave the land.

Ten—

O brave! the ten, 'tis very well!
There's none in love shall thee excel.
Only the maid who draws the ten
May wed, but nobody knows when.

King—

This noble king of diamonds shows
Thou long shalt live where pleasure flows;
But when a woman draws the king,
Sad, melancholy songs she'll sing.

Queen—

Now is the queen of diamonds fair,
She shows thou shalt some office share;
Oh, woman! if it fall to you,
Friends you will have not a few.

Knave—

Is now the knave of diamonds come?
Be sure beware the martial drum;
Yet if a woman draw the knave,
She shall much better fortune have.

HEARTS

Ace—

> He that draws the ace of hearts
> Shall surely be a man of parts;
> And she that draws it, I profess,
> Will have the gift of idleness.

Two—

> He who can draw the deuce shall be
> Endowed with generosity;
> But when a woman draws the card,
> It doth betide her cruel hard.

Three—

> The man who gets hold of this trey
> Always bound, always obey;
> A woman that shall draw this sort
> Will surely drink brandy by the quart.

Four—

> He that draws this four shall make
> A faithful love for conscience' sake;
> But if it's drawn by fair women,
> They will prove false, and that you'll find.

Five—

> Note that this five of hearts declares
> Thou shalt well manage great affairs;
> But if it's drawn by fair women,
> They sure will love all sorts of men.

Six—

> The six of heart's surely foretells
> Thou shalt be where great honor dwells;
> If it falls on the other side
> It then betokens scorn and pride.

Seven—

    Now this old seven, I'll maintain,
    Shows that thou hast not loved in vain;
    Thou shalt obtain the golden prize,
    But, with the maids, 'tis otherwise.

Eight—

    Having drawn the number eight,
    Shows thou'rt servile, born to wait;
    But if a woman draw the same,
    She'll mount upon the wings of fame.

Nine—

    By this long nine be well assured
    The lovesick pains must be endured;
    But the maid that draws this nine
    Soon in wedlock hands shall join.

Ten—

    This ten it is a lucky cast,
    For it doth show the worst is past;
    But if the maids the same shall have,
    Love will their tender hearts enslave.

King—

    By this card surely 'twill appear
    Thou shalt live long in happy cheer;
    And if a woman draw this card,
    She shall likewise be high preferred.

Queen—

    Now by this card it is well known
    Thou shalt enjoy still all thine own;
    But women, if they draw the same,
    Shall sure enjoy a happy name.

Knave—

> He that doth draw the knave of hearts
> Betokens he hath knavish parts;
> But if a woman draw the knave
> Of no man shall she be the slave.

SPADES

Ace—

> Thou that dost draw the ace of spades
> Shall be sore flouted by the maids;
> And when it is a damsel's lot,
> Both love and honor go to pot.

Two—

> Always this deuce betoken strife,
> And with a scolding, wicked wife;
> But if a woman's lot it be,
> Honor, great love and dignity.

Three—

> Thou that are happy in this trey
> Shalt surely wed a lady gay;
> Whilst maids who now the same shall take,
> Join marriage with a poor town rake.

Four—

> Now this same four betokens you
> Shall lead a dissipated crew;
> Maids that do draw the same shall meet
> With certain joys always complete.

Five—

> The five of spades gives you to know
> That you must through some troubles go;
> But, if a woman, it foretells
> Her virtue others' far excels.

Six—

The six foretells whene'er you wed
You'll find your expectations fled
But if a maid the number own
She'll wed a man of high renown.

Seven—

Now the seven comes to hand,
It does entitle you to land;
But maids with this shall wed with those
That have no money, friends, or clothes.

Eight—

This eight of spades foretells you shall
Wed a young maid fair, straight, and tall;
If to a maid the same shall come,
She weds the brother of Tom Thumb.

Nine—

Now by this nine thou are foretold,
Thou shalt wed one deaf, lame and old.
Females, when they draw this odd chance,
Shall of themselves to wealth advance.

Ten—

'Tis seen by this long ten of spades
That thou shalt follow many trades,
And thrive by none. But women, they
By this chance shall not work but play.

King—

By this brave king observe and note,
On golden streams you e'er shall float;
But women, by the self-same lot,
Shall long enjoy what they have got.

Queen—

  Here is the queen of spades likewise
  Thou soon shalt unto riches rise;
  A woman by the same shall have
  What her own heart doth sorely crave.

Knave—

  This is a knave, pray have a care
  That you fall not into despair.
  Women, who the same shall choose,
  Shall prove great flats, but that's no news!

CLUBS

Ace—

  He that doth draw the ace of clubs,
  From his wife gets a thousand snubs;
  But if maids do it obtain,
  It means that they shall rule and reign.

Two—

  Note that this deuce doth signify
  That thou a loyalist shalt die;
  The damsels that the same shall take
  Never will their good friends forsake.

Three—

  You that by chance this trey have drawn
  Shall on a worthless woman fawn.
  A maiden that shall draw this trey
  Shall be the lass that ne'er says nay.

Four—

  Now by this four we plainly see
  Four children shall be born to thee;
  And she that draws the same shall wed
  Two wealthy husbands, both well-bred.

Five—

Now by this five 'tis clear to see
Thy wife will but a slattern be.
This same five drawn by virgins, they
Shall all wed husbands kind and gay.

Six—

By this six thou'rt wed, we know,
To one that over thee will crow;
Maids that can draw the same shall be
Blest with good husbands, kind and free.

Seven—

Thou that hast now the seven drawn
Shall put thy Sunday clothes in pawn;
Maids that draw the same shall wear
Jewels rich without compare.

Eight—

By this club eight, tho' Whig or Tory,
Thy life will prove a tragic story;
Ye maids that draw the same are born
To hold both fools and fops in scorn.

Nine—

By this brave nine, upon my life,
You soon shall wed a wealthy wife;
She that shall draw the same shall have
One that is both fool and knave.

Ten—

Now for this number, half a score,
Shows that thou wilt be wretched poor;
Maids that can draw this number still
Shall have great joy and wealth at will.

King—
　　Here comes the king of clubs, and shows
　　Thou hast some friends as well as foes;
　　Maids that do draw this court card shall
　　Have very few, or none at all.

Queen—
　　If the queen of clubs thou hast,
　　Thou shalt be with great honor graced.
　　And women, if the same they find,
　　Will have things after their own mind.

Knave—
　　See how the surly knave appears!
　　Pray take care of both your ears!
　　Women, whene'er the same they see,
　　Will be what oft they used to be.

THE SIGNIFICANCE OF
QUARTETTES, TRIPLETS
AND PAIRS

Combinations of court cards—Combinations of plain cards—Various cards read together—General meaning of the several suits—Some lesser points to notice.

COMBINATIONS OF COURT CARDS

Four Aces—When these fall together they imply danger, financial loss, separation from friends, love troubles, and under some conditions imprisonment. The evil is mitigated in proportion to the number of them that are reversed.

Three Aces—Passing troubles, relieved by good news, faithlessness of a lover and consequent sorrow. If reversed, they mean foolish excess.

Two Aces—These portend union; if hearts and clubs it will be for good, if diamonds and spades, for evil, probably the outcome of jealousy. If one or both be reversed the object of the union will fail.

Four Kings—Honors, preferment, good appointments. Reversed, the good things will be of less value, but will arrive earlier.

Three Kings—Serious matters will be taken in hand with the best result unless any of the three cards be reversed, when it will be doubtful.

Two Kings—Co-operation in business, upright conduct and prudent enterprises to be crowned with success. Each one reversed represents an obstacle. All three reversed spell utter failure.

COMBINATION OF PLAIN CARDS

Four Queens—A social gathering which may be spoilt by one or more being reversed.

Three Queens—Friendly visits. Reversed, scandal, gossip and possibly bodily danger to the inquirer.

Two Queens—Petty confidences interchanged, secrets betrayed, a meeting between friends. When both are reversed there will be suffering for the inquirer resulting from his own acts. Only one reversed means rivalry.

Four Knaves—Roistering and noisy conviviality. Any of them reversed lessens the evils.

Three Knaves—Worries and vexations from acquaintances, slander calling the inquirer's honor in question. Reversed, it foretells a passage at arms with a social inferior.

Two Knaves—Loss of goods, malicious schemes. If both are reversed the trouble is imminent; if one only, it is near.

COMBINATIONS OF PLAIN CARDS

Four Tens—Good fortune, wealth, success in whatever enterprise is in hand. The more there are reversed, the greater number of obstacles in the way.

Three Tens—Ruin brought about by litigation. When reversed the evil is decreased.

Two Tens—Unexpected luck which may be connected with a change of occupation. If one is reversed it will come soon, within a few weeks possibly; if both are reversed it is a long way off.

Four Nines—Accomplishment of unexpected events. The number that are reversed stand for the time to elapse before the fulfillment of the surprise.

Three Nines—Health, wealth and happiness. Reversed, discussions and temporary financial difficulties caused by imprudence.

Two Nines—Prosperity and contentment, possibly accompanied by business matters, testamentary documents, and possibly a change of residence. Reversed, small worries.

Four Eights—Mingled success and failure attending a journey or the taking up of a new position. Reversed, undisturbed stability.

Three Eights—Thoughts of love and marriage, new family ties, honorable intentions. Reversed, flirtation, dissipation and foolishness.

Two Eights—Frivolous pleasures, passing love fancies, an unlooked-for development. Reversed, paying the price of folly.

Four Sevens—Schemes and snares, intrigue prompted by evil passions, contention and opposition. Reversed, small scores of impotent enemies.

Three Sevens—Sadness from loss of friends, ill-health, remorse. Reversed, slight ailments or unpleasant reaction after great pleasure.

Two Sevens—Mutual love, an unexpected event. Reversed, faithlessness, deceit or regret.

VARIOUS CARDS READ TOGETHER

The ten of diamonds next to the seven of spades means certain delay.

The ten of diamonds with the eight of clubs tells of a journey undertaken in the cause of love.

The nine of diamonds with the eight of hearts foretells for certain a journey.

The eight of diamonds with the eight of hearts means considerable undertakings; with the eight of spades there will be sickness; and with the eight of clubs there is deep and lasting love.

The seven of diamonds with the queen of diamonds tells of a very serious quarrel; with the queen of clubs we may look for uncertainty; with the queen of hearts there will be good news.

The ten of clubs followed by an ace means a large sum of money; should these two cards be followed by an eight and a king an offer of mariage is to be expected.

When the nine, ace, and ten of diamonds fall together we may look for important news from a distance; and if a court card comes out after them a journey will become necessary.

The eight and seven of diamonds in conjunction imply the existence of gossip and chatter to be traced to the inquirer.

When the king, queen, knave and ace of one color appear in sequence it is a sign of marriage; should the queen of spades and the knave of hearts be near, it shows there are obstacles in the way; the proximity of the eight of spades bodes ill to the couple in question but their happiness will be assured by the presence of the eight of hearts and the eight of clubs.

The ace of diamonds and the ten of hearts also foretell wedding bells.

The seven of spades, with either a court card or the two of its own suit, betrays the existence of a false friend.

The eight and five of spades coming together tell of jealousy that will find vent in malicious conduct.

A number of small spades in sequences are significant of financial loss, possibly amounting to ruin.

The king of hearts and the nine of hearts form a lucky combination for lovers.

The nine of clubs joined to the nine of hearts is indicative of affairs connected with a will likely to benefit the inquirer.

The queen of spades is the sign of widowhood, but if accompanied by the knave of her own suit she is symbolical of a woman who is hostile and dangerous to the inquirer.

GENERAL MEANING OF THE SEVERAL SUITS

Hearts, as might well be supposed, are specially connected with the work of Cupid and Hymen. The suit also has close reference to affairs of the home and to both the domestic and social sides of life.

Diamonds are mainly representative of financial matters small and great, with a generally favorable signification.

Clubs are the happiest omens of all. They stand for worldly prosperity, a happy home life with intelligent pleasures and successful undertakings.

Spades on the other hand forebode evil. They speak of sickness, death, monetary losses and anxieties, separation from friends and dear ones, to say nothing of the minor worries of life. They are also representatives of love unaccompanied by reverence or respect and appealing exclusively to the senses.

SOME LESSER POINTS TO NOTICE

When a number of court cards fall together it is a sign of hospitality, festive social intercourse and gaiety of all kinds.

Married people who seek to read the cards must represent their own life partner by the king or queen

of the suit they have chosen for themselves, regardless
of anything else. For example, a very dark man, the
king of spades, must consider his wife represented by
the queen of spades even though she may be as fair
as a lily and not yet a widow.

Bachelors and spinsters may choose cards to personify their lovers and friends according to their coloring.

Two red tens coming together foretell a wedding,
and two red eights promise new garments to the inquirer.

A court card placed between two cards of the same
grade—for instance, two nines, two sevens, etc., shows
that the one represented by that card is threatened
by the clutches of the law.

It is considered a good augury of success when, in
dealing the cards out, those of lesser value than the
knave are in the majority, especially if they are clubs.

Should a military man consult the cards he must
always be represented by the king of diamonds.

It is always essential to cut cards with the left
hand, there being a long-established idea that it is
more intimately connected with the heart than the
right. A round table is generally preferred by those
who are in the habit of practising cartomancy. It is
a matter of opinion as to whether the cards speak with
the same clearness and accuracy when consulted by
the inquirer without an intermediary. The services of
an adept are generally supposed to be of great advantage, even when people have mastered the rudi-
ments of cartomancy themselves.

Patience, the power of putting two and two together, a quick intuitive perception, and a touch of
mysticism in the character, are all useful factors in the
pursuit of this pastime.

THE COMBINATION
OF SEVENS

A method with selected cards—General rules—How to proceed—Reading of the cards—Signification of cards—Some combinations—A typical example—Further inquiries—The seven packs.

This method is very simple and, as it takes but a short time, is more suitable when there are many fortunes to read. A little practice will soon enable a would-be cartomancer to construe the various combinations, as there are so few cards to remember.

It may be objected that meanings are now given that are different from those taught in the first method. This is certainly a fact, but it also is an advantage; one method may suit one person's abilities and intuitiveness better than another, and so enable a more comprehensive reading to be given from the diminished pack than from the full Tarot pack.

GENERAL RULES

Thirty-two cards only are selected from an ordinary pack of playing cards. In each suit the ace, king, queen, knave, ten, nine, eight, and seven are retained; all the others, those from two to six inclusively, are discarded.

The cards must be shuffled and cut into three sections by the inquirer, each cut being turned face upwards. The manipulator must carefully note the result of these cuts, as they give an indication of what is coming. The center pack is to be taken first, the last next, and the first last of all.

Holding this newly arranged pack in the left hand, draw off three cards, and facing them upwards, select the highest card of any suit that may appear. Retain this one and put the others aside for the next deal. Proceed in this way until you have finished the pack, then shuffle all the discard together, and repeat until you have any number over twenty-one on the table. If three cards of any suit should appear, or three cards of the same value, they are all to be taken.

It must not be forgotten that the cards are also selected from the "cuts," and should the lifting of one card reveal another of greater value of the same suit exposed, then that also is retained.

HOW TO PROCEED

The first question to decide is which card will represent the inquirer. This is generally settled according to the complexion: diamonds for the very fair; hearts, those of medium coloring; clubs for brunettes with brown hair; and spades for those of dark complexion. This suit also represents elderly people. A king represents a man and a queen a woman. This representative card is not to be drawn out; it is shuffled with the others, and taken when it is the highest of its suit. The only exception to this rule is when there have been already twenty-one or more cards selected; then it must be taken from the remainder and placed last of all.

READING OF THE CARDS

The reading in this method is from left to right, and the cards are to be placed in a semicircle or horseshoe, in the order they are drawn.

Court cards represent people and the numbers relate to events. Generally diamonds relate to money and interest; hearts, to the affections; clubs, to business; spades, to the more serious affairs of life.

The signification of each card is given separately, as well as of some of the combinations, and an example of a fortune is worked out, the study of which will more easily enable a student to understand this method.

SIGNIFICATION OF CARDS

HEARTS

King	A man with brown hair and blue eyes
Queen	A woman of similar complexion
Knave	A friend with good intentions
Ten	Marriage
Nine	Wish
Eight	Affection
Seven	Friendship
Ace	Home

DIAMONDS

King	A fair man
Queen	A fair woman
Knave	A friend
Ten	Wealthy marriage
Nine	Rise in social position
Eight	Success with speculation

| Seven | A good income |
| Ace | A wedding or present of jewelry |

CLUBS

King	A man who is neither fair nor dark
Queen	A woman in middle life
Knave	A business friend
Ten	Journey by water
Nine	Successful business
Eight	Pleasure in society
Seven	A business affair
Ace	A letter, check, or legal document

SPADES

King	A dark man
Queen	A dark woman (or widow)
Knave	Personal thoughts
Ten	A journey by land
Nine	Illness or sorrow
Eight	A loss
Seven	A disagreement
Ace (right way)	Responsible position in the service of the Government.
Ace (upside down)	

SOME OF THE COMBINATIONS

Three kings—a new friend; two kings and a knave —meeting with an old friend; three knaves—legal business; three queens—a disagreement with women; three tens, very fortunate combination. If the ten of clubs and the ten of hearts appear with the ten of diamonds, it will easily be seen that a wealthy marriage will take place after a journey across the water.

Three nines—very speedy good news; three eights —a move; three sevens—speedy news, but not altogether satisfactory; three aces—very good fortune; the ace of clubs and the ace of diamonds would signify an offer of marriage by letter.

The ace and nine of hearts mean that you will have the realization of your heart's desire in your own house; the ace and nine of spades—that sorrow and death will come to your family; the king and queen of any suit, with the ten of hearts is a sign that you will hear of a marriage shortly.

A TYPICAL EXAMPLE

Now we will proceed to read a fortune and for the subject we will take the queen of hearts. The first shuffle and division of the pack into three reveals three hearts—king, knave, and seven—which indicates that the lady whom the queen represents has a firm male friend, who is neither fair nor dark. These three cards are taken and laid in order, beginning on the left hand.

Then the packs having been taken in order as described and held in the left hand, the fortune-teller proceeds to draw off three cards, and make his selection according to the rule. The pack being finished, the process is repeated twice more.

In three deals the fortune of the queen of hearts revealed the following cards, and if a student will take a pack of cards and select the same, he can judge how the various combinations may be read.

King, knave, seven of hearts, ace of clubs, king of spades, queen of clubs, queen of diamonds, queen of spades, king of clubs, knave of diamonds, ace of hearts, knave of spades, king of diamonds, knave of clubs, queen of hearts, ace of diamonds, ten of hearts, eight of clubs, seven of spades, ace of spades, ten of clubs, ten of spades, ten of diamonds.

Now, from the queen of hearts we will proceed to count seven, taking into consideration the way the lady's face is turned. It is to the left, consequently the seventh card from her is the queen of spades, the seventh from which is the king of hearts, and the seventh again is the ten of hearts. I read this that the lady has some good friends; but that the woman whom the queen of spades represents will resent her marriage but without effect. The next card is the knave of diamonds followed by the seven of hearts and the seven of spades—a combination which represents some speedy news, not exactly to the advantage of the inquirer. The knave of spades followed by the king and the ten of clubs denotes that a dark man, who is separated from the queen of hearts, is constantly thinking of her and hoping for a speedy reunion.

The knave of clubs and the queen of diamonds come next. Knaves and women form a conjunction that never brings good luck; but in this case they are followed by the ten of diamonds, one of the most fortunate cards in the pack. The ace of diamonds and the king of clubs follow which means an offer of marriage shortly. The queen of hearts is indeed a sad coquette, for there is no indication that she accepts this, as the knave of hearts with the eight of clubs and the ace of hearts are quickly on the scene. It appears that there is another wooer who comes to her home and is received with pleasure.

More serious affairs appear now; the ace of clubs with the ace of spades and the king of diamonds signify that the lady is likely to have some business with which a woman darker than herself is connected.

This will lead to a considerable journey which she will immediately take, as the card denoting this counts seven directly to her.

Now we will look at the cards as they lie on the table. For a reading taken at random they foretell a very good future. All the court cards and the aces and tens are out, with the seven of hearts and the eight of clubs, and all are cards of favorable import.

Three queens together generally betoken some mischief or scandal, but as they are guarded by kings it will probably not amount to much. The ace of diamonds and the ten of hearts placed so near the representative card would surely tell us of a forthcoming marriage except that the queen has her face turned away from it. The three tens placed as they are tell of prosperity after journeys by land and water.

Now we will pair the cards and see if any more meaning can be extracted from them. On land and on the water this lady will meet a rich man who will entertain a strong affection for her. I must not omit to mention that the cards are paired from the extreme ends of the horseshoe. Thus the king of hearts and the ten of diamonds, knave of hearts and ten of spades, etc. The business appears again, and a dark man seems to be in some perplexity. The three queens are not yet separated and are in closer connection with the inquirer than ever. Oh! There will be chatting over the teacups about a marriage. The fair damsel herself appears to be a little more inclined to matrimony, but the three knaves imply that she will have some difficulty in settling her affairs.

The two kings imply that she has some staunch friends and that the result will be quite satisfactory. A general reading gives the impression that the queen of hearts is of a lovable disposition and fond of society, as so many court cards came out and if the three queens meant a little gossip it was in a kindly spirit.

FURTHER INQUIRIES

There is another little ceremony to be gone through which will tell us if she is likely to have her "heart's desire" realized. The nine of hearts, which is the symbol of a wish, did not appear so she is apparently very cool and neutral. However, the other cards may tell us something.

The used cards are to be shuffled and cut once by the inquirer and she may wish for anything she likes during the process. Then the cards are laid out one at a time in seven packs—six packs in a semicircle, and one in the center—the cards of the last are to be turned face upwards, but none of the other cards are to be exposed until the end.

THE SEVEN PACKS

The seven packs represent respectively—"yourself," "your house," "what you expect," "what you don't expect," "a great surprise," "what is sure to come true," and "the wish."

The cards, having been shuffled and cut once, are dealt out in the manner described, and these are the combinations we get:—

First Pack—Queen of spades, queen of hearts, ten of clubs, seven of hearts.

Second—Ace of spades, knave of clubs, ace of diamonds and ten of spades.

Third—Knave of spades, king of diamonds, knave of hearts.

Fourth—Queen of clubs, seven of spades, king of spades.

Fifth—Ten of diamonds, eight of clubs, and queen of diamonds.

Sixth—King of hearts, ten of hearts, king of clubs.

Wish—Ace of hearts, knave of diamonds, ace of clubs.

The first pack represents to me the meeting of the inquirer with a dark or elderly woman for whom she has a strong affection. Water is crossed before that meeting takes place.

The second pack reads as if a dark man would offer a ring or a present of jewelry, and also that he is contemplating a journey by land. He is probably a professional man, or in government service.

The third pack, with its combination of knaves and king, has reference to business transactions which will most probably be favorable to the interests of the queen.

The fourth pack presages some slight disappointment, illness or unhappiness in connection with some friends.

The fifth pack tells us that some brilliant fortune is awaiting a fair friend that will lead to a higher social position.

The sixth pack tells us that perhaps our seemingly indifferent queen of hearts has a slight tenderness for someone. He is older than she is and is only waiting for an opportunity to declare his affection. If the wish related to such a man as I have described, she may be certain of its fulfillment even should there be a slight delay.

The seventh or wish pack is extremely good, and tells us that many affairs will be transacted in writing.

The future of the queen of hearts is fair and bright,

her disposition is lovable and she will bring happiness to other people.

This example is not made up of selected cards. They were shuffled, cut and drawn in the ordinary way. I say this because so few cards of bad import have appeared and it might be thought these were chosen in order to avoid prophesying disappointments.

In the foregoing example twenty-three cards were dealt out, but the number may vary. It must, however, be an uneven number. Sometimes only fifteen or seventeen cards are taken, and with the smaller quantity of selected cards there is an optional way of concluding operations. After having read the pairs, the cards are gathered up, shuffled and cut into three packs instead of seven. These three are placed in a row, and a fourth card is put apart for the surprise. The inquirer is requested to choose one of the three packs, which represent respectively For the house, For those who did not expect it, and For the inquirer —the last being decided by the choice of the person in question.

When these three packs have been duly read, all the cards are again taken up except The Surprise (which is left face downwards on the table), and dealt out again, the same process being repeated three times until there are three cards set aside for the surprise. These are read last of all and form the concluding message to the inquirer. Let's hope it may be a cheerful one!

PALMISTRY

CHAPTER I

It is usual to divide the science of palmistry into two principal sections: Cheirognomy, or the science of interpreting the characters and instincts of men from the outward formations and aspects of their hands; and Cheiromancy, or the science of reading the characters and instincts of men, their actions and habits and the events of their past, present and future lives, in the lines and formations of the palms of their hands.

The first of these branches is the modern and more scientific one. It is really the easiest to master and to practice and though less interesting than the second is absolutely indispensable to a proper study of the lines of the palm. Master the subject of the general formation of hands, and you are well on the way to a mastery of the art of reading palms.

Terms Used

The traditional names of the planets are used with such frequency in palmistry that their general significance should be familiar.

Jupiter, the largest of the planets, was named after the Greek god known to the Romans as Jupiter. Jupiter was the king of gods, a ruler, mighty and powerful over gods and men; yet he was kind, noble, and magnanimous.

Saturn, the name of the second planet, was the name of a god of the earth, father of other gods. He is represented as an melancholy old man with long fingernails, dressed in old clothes, and fond of grubbing in the ground. His hair is long and uncut, his features thin and haggard, his head stooped; but in his lonely way he is very imaginative, and has a poetic fancy of the melancholy order.

Mars is the strong god of war. He is red—often red-headed—full-blooded, passionate, and active. He is the energetic god, and in astrology his planet (which shines with a red light) is supposed to give a fiery temper, both in love and combat.

Venus, the chief female deity and planet, is the goddess of love. She is full and round, gentle and beautiful, fond of music, dancing and art. She admires the god Mars, though the reverse of active herself. She appreciates harmonious colors and all forms of luxury. At times she is voluptuous in the extreme.

Apollo is the sun god. He is represented as a handsome young man, as perfectly beautiful as Venus but thoroughly masculine and never voluptuous. He too understands harmony of sound and color and beautiful lines. Like Jupiter, he is also noble and lofty in thought and purpose.

Mercury is the messenger of the gods. His planet circles the sun in a shorter time than any other. He is always on the wing. He is the god of merchants sending ships to the ends of the earth, and of all ready talkers, liars, and even thieves. He is indispensable to business success, and gives everything that is clever, smart, brisk and up to the minute; also oratory.

Luna, or the Moon, is dreamy, poetic, and sympathetic. She likes to be nursed by a strong arm. She understands the sufferings and struggles of all around her, cares for the sick, and will talk quietly by the hour in the faint twilight or before the evening fire. She is also a great traveler. She must wander, and in a fit of depression she may even commit suicide.

Names of the Fingers

The index finger is named for Jupiter;

The middle finger for Saturn;

The ring finger for Apollo;

The little finger for Mercury.

The large fleshy bunch under the thumb, in the palm of the hand, is called the Mount of Venus.

The large fleshy bunch on the other side of the hand (that is, the outer side of the palm), is called the Mount of Luna, or the Moon.

Mars is represented by the mount on the middle of the outer side of the palm, just below Luna, and above the mount at the base of the little finger, known as the Mount of Mercury. He also governs the triangular plane in the center of the palm.

CHAPTER II

In this chapter we deal with the gastronomics of the various types of subjects, *i.e.*, those who have the special mounts and fingers dominant.

JUPITERIANS—Large eaters and drinkers, with a firm, stout appearance. Punctual meals consisting of a long menu, handsomely served. Prefer rich and full-flavored foods, chops and steaks, luxuries, especially expensive things "out of season."

In Excess—Extravagance to wastefulness.

Favorite Dishes and Drinks—Turtle soup; turbot, trout; entrees highly spiced with cloves, mace, nutmeg, etc.; beef, mutton, venison; turkey, duck; plum and other rich puddings; parsnips, French beans; Stilton cheese; pears, plums, figs, olives, mulberries, raspberries, walnuts; stout, port, punch, spirits, liquors (cherry brandy, sloe gin, etc.); coffee.

SATURNIANS—Moderate eaters and drinkers with thin, muscular appearance. Indifferent about the time and serving of their frugal fare. Prefer very mild-flavored foods and all kinds of vegetables (sometimes vegetarians).

In Excess—Ascetics.

Favorite Dishes and Drinks—Stewed eels, cod; cold meats; eggs; milk pudding; stewed fruits; all kinds of vegetables, salads; Dutch and cream cheese; medlars; water, cocoa.

APOLLO SUBJECTS—Very moderate eaters and drinkers; can miss a meal with equanimity; content with short menu but tastefully served. Prefer highly flavored food—game, entrees, savories, and casseroles.

In Excess—Epicureans.

Favorite Dishes and Drinks—Oxtail soup; salmon, mullet; all kinds of entrees and savories; hare, pheasant, partridge, and all small game; rich cakes, biscuits; peas, beet-root; Gruyere cheese; peaches; apricots, greengages, oranges, ginger, Brazil nuts; light wines, liquors (*e.g.*, Chartreuse).

MERCURIANS—Moderate but rapid eaters and temperate drinkers, with spare and wiry appearance. Irritable if kept waiting for their meals, which consist of short menus served without much ceremony. Prefer plain foods, as meat and two vegetables, plenty of bread and plain puddings.

In Excess—Gobblers.

Favorite Dishes and Drinks—Fried rice, smoked haddock; joints, steaks, chops; roast fowl; plain puddings; bitter vegetables (*e.g.*, spinach, seakale, and turnips); Gorgonzola cheese; all kinds of raw fruits; filberts; ale, sherry, claret, and sparkling water.

MARTIANS—Voracious eaters and large drinkers, with rather massive appearance. Ready for a meal at any time, consisting of short but substantial menu. Prefer strong-flavored and pungent foods served very hot (temperature), and all condiments.

In Excess—Gourmands.

Favorite Dishes and Drinks—Mulligatawny soups; no fresh fish; kippers, bloaters, fish pastes; curries and hot savories; all salt meats; pickles; goose; fruit tarts, pastries; brown bread; cabbage, beans, carrots, onions, garlic, horseradish, radishes, mustard and cress, watercress; Cheddar and American cheeses; chestnuts; beer and spirits.

LUNA SUBJECTS—Variable appetites but large drinkers, with loose, fleshy appearance. No stated time for meals, and not particular how they are served. Prefer liquid foods (soups, purees, stews, etc.)

In Excess—Intemperance.

Favorite Dishes and Drinks—Soups; all kinds of fresh fish, oysters, crab, and lobster; purees, Irish stew; no sweets; marrow, lettuce, cucumber, mushrooms; watermelon; drinks of all kinds.

VENUSIANS—Small eaters, with correctly portioned appearance. Fairly punctual to light menu daintily served. Prefer delicately flavored foods, sweets (puddings) and bonbons.

In Excess—Faddy or greedy.

Favorite Dishes and Drinks—White soup; sole; veal, lamb; rabbit, chicken; all kinds of fancy puddings; potatoes, tomatoes, asparagus; Camembert cheese; apples, grapes, strawberries; almonds, ciders, champagne, liquors (*e.g.*, Benedictine); tea.

CHAPTER III

The Elementary Hand

First, with the eye, or better by means of a ruler, measure the length of the fingers at the back, from the center of the knuckle of the longest finger to its tip; then measure the palm from the highest opening between any two fingers, and the first line running around the wrist, or the point where in your judgment the palm ends and the wrist begins.

The length of the fingers should be greater in all cases than the length of the palm, or at any rate about the same. In the lower animals and the lower orders of men the palm is longer than the fingers, till the fingers become little more than toes, and the nails grow over the ends of the fingers like claws.

The Elementary hand has short fingers, the skin is coarse and often hard, though not always, and the palm thick and chubby. The thumb is short, thick and usually square at the end. Persons with such a hand have no control over their passions and have little mind or capacity for education. They are brutes and like brutes may commit murder in a drunken passion. Like brutes too, they may be amiable though never very appreciative of others, and may grow rich through their activity in the lower planes of life. The pure type

of Elementary hand is rarely found in civilized countries, though something approaching it is not un-
common.

Scientific Types

Every one has noticed how differently shaped are the
fingertips of all persons of education and intellectual
power. These differences have caused cheirologists to
divide hands into classes, which represent corresponding types of character. The ancient teachers considered
that there were seven of these classes, because they also
reckoned seven planets and seven temperaments, etc.
The modern palmists teach that there are three natural
divisions, the Conical, Spatulate and Square; and two
smaller classes contained within the three principal
types but with peculiarities of their own, the Extreme
Pointed, and the Mixed Type.

"Pure types," that is, fingers entirely conic, spatulate
or square, are seldom met with. We must master the
simple types, however, and learn to combine their
qualities when we find the types themselves combined
in any particular hand.

The Conic Type represents Ideality.

The Spatulate repreesnts Action.

The Square represents Reason.

The Conic Hand

The Conic hand has long eliptical nails, not very
large, but delicate, and the whole hand corresponds.
The fingers are long and tapering, the palm by no
means thick, and the skin is usually smooth and clear.
Subjects with conical-shaped tips to their fingers dream
rather than act, especially if the hand is generally soft.
"People with the Conic hand are often, in fact,

designated 'the children of impulse'. There is a great
variety in connection with this type, but it is more
usually found as a full, soft hand with pointed fingers
and rather long nails. Such a formation denotes an
artistic, impulsive nature but one in which love of
luxury and indolence predominate."

Persons possessing this type of hand are usually brilliant, clever and gifted as musicians or artists, especially
if the ring finger, the finger of Apollo, is proportionately long. They often fail, however, because of lack
of application and a willingness for hard work.

The Spatulate Hand

The Spatulate hand has fingertips like a druggist's
spatule, or ladle. The ends of their fingers seem ab-
normally developed by constant work on details. Persons possessing this type are the workers of the world.
They carry out the ideas of the conical type. The thumb
must always be large. "The great pronounced characteristics of this type are: action, movement, energy;
and, of course, the harder or firmer the hand the more
pronounced will these characteristics be. A man of this
type is resolute, self-confident, and desirous of abun-
dance rather than of sufficiency. In love he will be more
constant and faithful than the conic or pointed-handed
subject, by reason of his want of inclination toward
things romantic and poetic. With a small thumb the
spatulate subject will try to do much, but will fail,
through want of perserverance and uncertainty in his
course of action." Persons of this class are fond of order
and regularity, and are always doing something. They
are strict and even tyrannical, but always just. If the
palm be hard, they will work themselves; if soft, they
make others do the work; but action of some sort is a
necessity and they are restless when forced to be idle.

The Square Hand

The Square hand has nails more or less square at the ends, and the fingertips are nearly square. The hand itself is broad, and the palm is nearly square, especially at the wrist and at the base of the fingers. Usually the joints are rather large, especially the joints nearest the palm, the thumb with the root well developed, the palm itself of medium thickness, hollow, and rather firm. The whole hand is usually a very large one.

Such a hand is often known as the useful hand, since it is so common in the useful walks of life. Carpenters and mechanics of all kinds, inventors, architects (especially builders of useful buildings), and in fact everyone engaged in a strictly useful occupation that also requires intelligence and reasoning judgment possesses this hand.

Possessors of square hands (as may be seen by the knotted joints) are thinkers; they must have a reason for everything. They do not work so hard as those with spatulate fingertips, but they will probably accomplish more. They have very little sympathy with the beautiful in any form, especially when it is not also useful, and despise persons with conic fingers. They are preeminently the world's scientists as opposed to the world's artists and poets. "They are sincere and true in promise, staunch in friendship, strong in principle, and honest in business. Their greatest fault is that they are inclined to reason by a twelve-inch rule, and disbelieve all they cannot understand." "The best musicians (composers and theorists) have always delicately squared fingers with slightly developed joints and small thumbs." Perhaps this explains why the great musical composers are Germans. Singers and performers on violin and piano are more likely to have conic hands, with enough of the square type to give them perseverance in practice.

The Mixed Hand

The Mixed hand as a type is so called because it has distinct characteristics of several of the three elementary types we have just been considering. The nail on one finger may be square, that on another may be conic, and that on a third spatulate; there may be square nails and fingertips on long, tapering fingers, or conic nails and tapering fingers on square palms. The Mixed hand must be judged first of all by the prevailing type. That is, if two or more of the fingers are spatulate, the type is mixed spatulate; if two or more are conical, it is mixed-conical; if two or more are square, it is mixed-square. Each finger should be read separately, and then the balance carefully adjusted.

A pointed or conic Jupiter always gives the love of reading and perception, and modifies the sterner qualities of the other fingers. Thus the argumentativeness of the square fingers may be modified by the tact of a long-pointed Mercury; while a pointed hand with a square Saturn has the saving grace of prudence to correct its vagaries.

All palmists agree that the mixed hand is the most difficult to read, and at the same time it is the most common. "It is the hand of ideas, of versatility, and generally of changeability of purpose. A man with such a hand is adaptable to both people and circumstances, clever, but erratic in the application of his talents. He will be brilliant in conversation, be the subject science, art or gossip. The best chance they have of becoming really distinguished is to take the best talent they have and cultivate that one to the exclusion of the others;

but they seldom have the strength of purpose to effect this."

Other Types

The old palmists describe two other types, the Philosophic and the Psychic already spoken of as the Exaggerated Conic.

The Philosophic are divided into two classes or sections; one that of the materialists whose ideas are derived from external influences, and the other that of the idealists whose ideas are evolved from their inner consciousness.

The distinguishing characteristic of these hands is the knotted joints of the fingers. The first joint, or that nearest the fingertips, if well developed gives the idealistic class, or those whose reasoning and philosophy is concentrated on mental subjects; the second joint, or that nearest the palm, if well developed gives the materialistic class, or those whose reasoning and philosophy is concentrated on physical and material matters.

The hand with knotted joints (in English countries) usually belongs to the college professor or scientist. Persons with such a hand glean wisdom, but seldom gather gold. They are students rather than workers. As a matter of fact, the knotted joints may belong to the conic, the square, or the spatulate type of hand and so this is not properly a separate type. Moreover, in common life it is a type peculiar to Oriental nations, especially to India. "In character they are silent and secretive; they are deep thinkers, careful over little matters, even in the use of little words; they are proud with the pride of being different from others; they rarely forget an injury, but they are patient with the patience of power."

The Psychic or Exaggerated Conic hand is still more
rarely found. It is the "most beautiful and delicate, but,
alas! the most useless and impractical type of hand."
This type of hand is very small and delicate, having a
thin palm, fine fingers, long and delicately pointed, or
with joints only just indicated by a very slight swelling.
It has generally a pretty little thumb. To these subjects
belong the domains of the beautiful ideal, the land of
dreams, of Utopian ideas and of artistic fervor; they
have the delicacy and true instinct of art of the conic
hand, but without its sensualism, its egotism and its
worldliness. The luxurious dreaming Orientals are almost exclusively of this type. Among them we find
spiritualists, mediums, and many persons who prove
the easy prey of impostors. In countries where such
hands predominate and hold the reins of government,
we find that rule is maintained by superstition, by
priests and by fetishism.

Such subjects are ruled by heart and by soul; their
feelings are acute, their nerves highly strung, and they
are easily fired with a wondrous enthusiasm. Theirs are
the talents which produce the most inspired poetry.
But in our material Western world the possessors of
such hands are invariably classed as failures. To their
own hearts, however, their lives are anything but
failures in spite of the fact that suicide is not uncom-
mon among them.

CHAPTER IV

We have considered the types of nails and fingertips
under the head of Types of Hands. There are, however,
many special points to be considered in connection
with the fingers.

Length of Fingers

If the fingers looked at from the front (not measured from the back as previously described) appear to be short, the subject will be found to be impulsive, hasty, quick in thought and action, and inclined to regard the whole of a subject rather than trouble about details.

Long fingers love detail, and are constantly inclined to curiosity, worry and fidgetiness.

A well balanced character will have the fingers and palm of equal length (or they will appear to be in good proportion). Such a person will appreciate the wide sweep of the horizon, and yet note lovingly the daisies 'neath our feet.

FINGERS

JUPITER (index finger).

Good.	*Too short.*
Love of rule.	Dislike of Responsibility.
Too long.	*Crooked.*
Tyranny.	Lack of honor.

SATURN (middle finger)

Prudence.	Frivolity.
Morbidity.	Hysteria.

APOLLO (ring finger).

Love of the beautiful.	No artistic sense.
Love of speculation (gambling).	False ideas of art.

MERCURY (little finger).

General capacity.	No executive ability.
Craft.	Wanting in business tact.

General Shape of Fingers

A finger is said to be "good" when it is straight, well developed, and in proportion to the other fingers; "bad" when it is too long or too short, twisted, crooked or bent.

When the hand is held palm upward, and one finger appears to stand up, that is said to be the dominant finger and will give the keynote of the character. The qualities indicated by the different fingers will thus vary in degree with the power of that finger, and must be judged accordingly. The following table gives the chief qualities to be deduced from each finger:

Fingers set evenly on a line above the mounts are said to indicate success.

Any finger set below the others loses some of its power. Mercury low-set shows that circumstances are against the subject and that life will be a struggle. If Apollo is set lower than Saturn, the artistic faculties will not receive their full cultivation. Saturn is seldom displaced.

Large and Small Hands

A large hand indicates a love and appreciation of details and minutiae; a medium-sized hand denotes comprehension of details and power of grasping a whole; while very small hands betray always the instincts and appreciation of synthesis. The large-handed subject will have things small in themselves, but exquisitely finished, while the small-handed subject desires the massive, the grandiose, and the colossal. Artists in horology have always large hands, while the designers and builders of pyramids and colossal temples have always small hands. In Egyptian papyri and hieroglyphic inscriptions the smallness of the hands of the persons represented always strikes one at first sight. In like manner persons with small hands always write large, while people with large hands always write (naturally) small.

The Phalanges

The phalanges are the divisions of the fingers and thumb between the joints, and are reckoned downward from that containing the nail, as first, second and third.

First, the ideal; second, the intellectual and third, the material.

The first phalanx shows the type, and consequently the class to which the hand belongs.

Pointed—The subject imagines, but does not execute (Ideality.)

Spatulate—Practicality (Action).

Square—Desire for reason in all things.

In the case of the Mixed hand, the phalanges of the different fingers will vary, and one will modify the other. Thus a pointed first phalanx of Jupiter in an otherwise square hand gives perception of the ideal, which will modify a little the hardness of the square fingers. The following table will show these variations at a glance:

JUPITER

Conic	*Spatulate.*
Perception.	Lack of Perception.
Square.	
Bluntness.	

SATURN

Frivolity.	Prudence.
Morbidness.	

APOLLO

Unpractical art.   Movement in art
                                         (drama).

Reality in art.

MERCURY

Tact.   Business management.
                Lack of tact.

JUPITER

First phal. long.   *Second phal. long.*
Superstition.   Ambition.
                Third phal. long.
                Desire to rule.

SATURN

Melancholy.   Love of agriculture.
                Economy.

APOLLO

Love of art (sense of   Intellectual art.
form—wide shows
    color sense).
                (With long straight
                headline) Avarice.

MERCURY

Power of words   Business capacity.
(In excess, lying.)
                Love of display.

The first phalanges long in proportion to the others
show constructive ability (ideas in action).

The second phalanges long in proportion show a
desire for intellectual life.

The third phalanges long in proportion and thick show a desire for material pleasures. When these phalanges are especially thick, they show self-pleasing, greediness, love of eating and drinking, and, if very soft and full, a love of smoking.

If these phalanges are cut away at the sides, the subject is fastidious but not greedy. If they are flat and unremarkable, then the pleasures of the table have no attractions; the subject can "rough it" with enjoyment. A deep cut at the base of the third phalanx is said to indicate shyness.

The above table showed the effect of a long phalanx in any part of any finger.

Inclination of the Fingers

If all the fingers turn toward Saturn there will be an excess of melancholy in the life. The following table will show at a glance the various effects:

JUPITER

Leaning toward thumb gives great desire for independence.
Leaning toward Saturn gives morbid pride.

SATURN

Leaning toward Jupiter gives superstitious sadness.
Leaning toward Apollo gives less morbidity, more imagination.

APOLLO

Leaning toward Saturn gives morbid vanity.

Leaning toward Mercury gives commercial art ("pot-boilers").

Stretch of the Fingers

An extra large stretch

Between Jupiter and the thumb gives generosity.

Between Jupiter and Saturn gives independence of thought.

Between Saturn and Apollo gives independence of circumstances ("happy-go-lucky").

Between Apollo and Mercury gives independence of action—Bohemianism.

All the fingers falling easily and wide apart indicates unconventionality.

Lines of the Phalanges

Straight lines on the phalanges are good, showing success; transverse lines show obstacles.

A deep line running up the third and second phalanges of Jupiter signifies some pet ambition—from the rest of the hand this may be easily demonstrated.

Transverse lines on the third phalanx are said to show money by inheritance.

A straight line running up Saturn shows military glory. Tradition connects this finger with mining operations; two parallel lines show success.

A straight line up the finger of Apollo shows marked success. A half circle on the third phalanx shows misfortune.

Confused lines on the third phalanx of Mercury show deception. A circle or half-circle on the second phalanx indicates a thief.

Three lines running straight up the finger show the tendency to be ever seeking for a "mares' nest."

One line on Mercury shows scientific success.

A crooked line like a furrow crossing the lower phalanx shows astuteness—especially in self-defense.

Many small lines on all the phalanges show delicate health.

The Joints of the Fingers

When the joints are so developed as to cause a perceptible bulge they are said to be knotted. Fingers on which the joints cannot be readily seen are said to be smooth. Knotted fingers may have both joints developed, or only one.

The joints or knots are the distinguishing mark of the philosophic type of hand. If the first joint (that nearest the nail) is developed it indicates a well-ordered mind, a mind that will find a reason for all its theories and all its actions. Nothing is taken for granted, nothing accepted without proof, in religion, in science or in art. The subjects are in consequence often discontented and skeptical, ever seeking their ideals and never finding them in this world.

When the upper joints are well developed, a large amount of talent is indicated; but we shall have to look to other parts of the hand to see with what success the talent is used.

The second joint, or that nearest the palm, is called the joint of material order. With a soft palm the subject will like to see other people "tidying up"; with the hard, energetic palm they will put things in their proper place themselves.

If both joints are well developed, the instincts of the subject will be symmetry, order and punctuality. There will be a strong inclination toward the sciences.

The development of the second joint only gives

order in material and selfish matters and makes merchants, calculators and speculators.

With smooth fingers (that is, neither joint developed), proceedings and actions will be governed by inspiration and by impulse, by sentiment and by fancy rather than, as in the former case, by reasoning, knowledge and analysis, and whatever the type of the hand, if the fingers are smooth the first impression of the subject is always the correct one, and subsequent reflections will not help in arriving at a conclusion.

The development of the third joint, or knuckle, has not received much attention from palmists, but the members of the Cheirological Society of London call it the "knot of domestic order." It is often found in the hands of fussy housekeepers who can never let well enough alone and are always fidgeting to have everything clean.

The presence of knots checks enthusiasm. Subjects having the first knot developed on Jupiter only are skeptical with regard to religious matters only.

The Nails

The color of the nails shows whether the circulation is good or not. If they are dark, the circulation is bad. Sometimes they will be fairly purple. This is an indication of temporary ill-health.

Bright red nails indicate a hot temper, pink nails a hasty temper, and white nails a calm temper. If the color lies in bands of pink and white, the temper is intermittent and depends on the nerves and the state of health. Large nails feel more lasting anger than small ones. Short nails show mockery and criticism. "Almond" or "filbert" nails, if pink, are often peevish; if white, indifferent.

Flat nails show some tendency to paralysis.

Fluted nails (those with small ridges running from top to bottom) show backache and spinal trouble.

Ridges across the nails show an illness.

White specks show nervousness, or a temporary condition of nervous exhaustion, or slight illness.

Round nails are said to show a tendency to tuberculosis. (This means roundness from side to side the whole length of the nail.)

A square base indicates a desire for revenge.

Soft rounded base indicates amiability.

Wedge-shaped base indicates quickness to take offense and feel slights.

Very long nails much curved in any direction show a weak physical constitution and tendency to throat and lung trouble.

Short nails curved and fluted would show merely throat trouble.

Short and small nails in general show tendency toward heart disease. Large moons indicate a good circulation, small moons heart disease. Short nails inclined to lift or curve up at the edges because they are so flat indicate serious nerve disease and paralysis, especially if they are patched with white and are brittle.

Long nails indicate calmness and resignation and their owners take things easily. Long nails show an artistic nature and great ideality and a tendency to be visionary. Short-nailed persons, on the contrary, are extremely critical, inclined to logic, reason and facts. They are quicker, sharper and keener in judgment than the long-nailed people, and have a keener sense of humor and the ridiculous. If nails are broader than they are long they show a pugnacious disposition and a tendency to worry and meddle with other people's business.

General Characteristics of the Fingers

If the fingers are thick they show love of ease and luxury.

If when the fingers are held together and the hand is looked at toward the light, spaces sufficient to let the light pass can be seen between the bases of the fingers, generosity is indicated; if the fingers fit tightly together avarice and extreme selfishness are to be read.

Twisted and badly formed fingers with few lines in the palms show a tyrannical and cruel, if not a murderous disposition.

Hands which open and close very stiffly betray stubborness.

People whose fingers have a tendency to turn back, being supple and elastic, are generally sagacious and clever, though inclined to extravagance. They are always curious and inquisitive.

If the little fleshy ball or pad is found on the face of the first phalanx it is a sign of sensitiveness and sensibility toward other people, and consequently tact (due to a fear of giving pain) and taste (the natural possession of sensitive people).

CHAPTER V

The Thumb

First Phalanx, Will; Second Phalanx, Logic; Third Phalanx, Love—The Setting of the Thumb.

The thumb is perhaps the most important single member of the manyfold hand. It gives the keynote of the whole character, and therefore merits a chapter by itself.

The three phalanges show respectively:

First (nail), will.

Second (middle), logic.
Third (part of palm), love.

First Phalanx—Will

If the first phalanx is long, firm to the touch and spatulate, the will will be constant and little affected by the opinions of others. If the point is soft and tapering, even if very long, the power of the will is unused and the subject is swayed by others. If heavy, almost clubbed, we find unreasoning obstinacy. If the thumb is very supple and turns far back we read generosity that in extreme cases goes to extravagance, even to complete lack of honor in the matter of spending money. Suppleness of the whole thumb is said to be a sign of dramatic talent. A depression in the center of the first phalanx shows susceptibility to flattery.

Second Phalanx—Logic

If the second phalanx is long, strong and proportionately developed it shows the power of abstract reasoning, of seeing all sides of an argument. It checks enthusiasm, and with a small first phalanx gives indecision. Such people give good advice but do not follow it themselves. "Waisted," that is, cut away at the sides, there is the power to see only one side of the question and it reduces all argument to a personal matter. "The finer formation of the thumb being the indication of the greater development of the intellectual will, and the coarse formation that of the nature that will use more brute force in the accomplishment of an object, it follows that the waist-like appearance, which is a portion of the finer development, indicates the tact born of mental power, whereas the fuller, coarser development indicates force in the carrying out of a purpose, in keeping with the characteristics of each nature."

Third Phalanx—Love

The part of the third phalanx lying outside the Mount of Venus, shows the power of the emotion. If combined with a heavy Mount of Venus we get sensuality. If this phalanx is long and clear, the passions are more ideal; if short and thick they are earthly. If the outer angle of the second joint is acute, a good ear for music is said to be indicated. The second joint is associated especially with time, the third with tune.

The Setting of the Thumb

If the thumb is set very high and straight it shows lack of adaptability and care for money to the verge of meanness. If it is high set and the first phalanx turns back, the subject spends money on himself.

When all the phalanges of the thumb are well balanced, strong and long, constancy of purpose is shown. A good, well-developed thumb can entirely redeem an otherwise bad hand, by bringing the modifying power of personal will to bear upon the inherited tendencies, making the idle energetic from conviction that labor brings the highest good; the self-indulgent temperate, because reason shows the healthful result of abstinence.

On the other hand, a weak, illogical thumb can render every talent otherwise shown in the hand useless. The small top phalanx and the small size of the whole member show the fickle, obstinate yet weak minded individual—lacking perseverance and absolutely unreliable. Nothing is brought to perfection, and the mind, swayed by the opinion of the last speaker, is incapable of sustained effort.

Small-thumbed people are governed more by the heart, large-thumbed by the head.

"When the first or nail phalanx is thick and heavy, with a short, flat nail, it is a sure indication of the ungovernable passion of the subject. All brutal natures have this clubbed formation."

Supple-jointed thumbs show moral irresponsibility. They are the impulsive children of nature who do not stop to think whether a thing is right or wrong.

The thumb carried habitually turned under the fingers shows a sensitive disposition.

CHAPTER VI

The Palm

Hair on the Back of the Hand—Color of the Hands.

The size of the palm must be judged by comparison with the fingers. No special measurements can be given, but a little practice will soon teach the student the right proportions. It should be measured from the base of the second finger to the first line of the bracelet.

A narrow palm belongs to the conventional hand, with fingers set closely together. Its narrowness generally consists in the small development of the mounts of *Mercury, Mars* and the *Moon;* and we therefore find that people with these narrow palms lack cheerfulness, pluck and imagination. Sometimes the thumb is pressed closely toward the hand and makes it appear narrow. This limits the stretch and prevents spontaneous generosity.

A square palm gives love of fresh air—if hard and flat a tendency toward outdoor sports.

A wide palm shows a good development of all the mounts.

When the palm is flat and lies on a level with the surrounding mounts, it shows that the Plain of *Mars* is developed, fighting and aggressive powers are used, and circumstances, however outwardly unfavorable, are forced in the end to yield.

Far different is the result of the hollow palm. With a lack of aggressiveness, drifting whither circumstances seem to lead, easily daunted, these characters need the sustaining moral force of a stronger nature to urge them to combat. Should a child's hand have this peculiarity he should never be snubbed; each effort should be encouraged and attempts made toward personal action should never be ridiculed. These hollow palms belong to sensitive minds to whom a breath of ridicule is a poison wind, stunting all growth and retarding every effort.

The consistency of the palm is also a very important factor in delineating a hand. When firm, even if in appearance it is soft, it will show energy, but not aggressive activity—of mind rather than of body.

When hard, flat and firm we have the fighting animal, never yielding, always doing—resistless energy and restless mind.

When the palm is soft and flabby we find indolence and laziness, which is accentuated and united with a love of luxury in food and life. When the back of the hand is also fat and the third phalanx much developed these people will always like others to do their work for them; even thinking is frequently too much trouble.

When these fat hands and thick fingers have a palm which feels firm to the touch, then their energy will expend itself chiefly on the gratification of their own gastronomic faculties. "Dinner" will be the one thing to live for.

A thin palm even when flat denotes delicate health; a firm, not too large one, warm to the touch, hard but not unduly so, good health; a thick, clumsy palm shows the preponderance of the animal instincts, brute force and egotism.

A thick palm is the characteristic of those for whom the alphabet consists of one letter—the capital "I"— while the flexible palm will generally show an adaptable character, fond of variety and change.

"The soft hand has more poetry in its composition than the hard. Thus, an artist with hard hands will paint things real and actual rather than ideal, and his pictures will be more active and manly than those of a softer-handed artist, who will paint the images of his fancy, and whose works will show greater soul, greater diversity and more fantasy.

"Again, a spatulate subject with hard hands will engage in active exercise, athletics and the like, while the similar but softer-handed subject prefers to watch others engaged in active occupations.

"Again, people with soft hands have always a love of the marvelous, being more nervous, more impressionable, more imaginative than those with hard hands. A very soft hand has a still greater degree of fascination for the strange and uncanny, being rendered additionally superstitious of bodily laziness. The tendency is still more pronounced if the fingers are pointed.

"Soft hands are often more capable of tenderness and affection than true love; but hard hands are generally the more capable of true love, though less prone to demonstrative tenderness and affection."

To be perfect, a hand should be firm without hardness, elastic without being flabby; such a hand hardens only very slowly with age, whereas an already firm

hand often becomes extremely hard. Smoothness and
a gentle firmness of the hand in youth betoken delicacy of mind, while dryness and thinness betray rude-
ness and insensibility.

The wrinkles on the hand should also be noticed. A
soft wrinkled hand shows impressionability and up-
rightness of soul, and a wrinkled hard hand is that of
a person who is pugnacious, irritating and teasing,
especially if the nails be short.

The back of the hand lined and wrinkled always
indicates benevolence of mind and sensitiveness of
soul.

The man with the firm, strong hands and the developed Mount of Venus is the man who will exert himself to amuse others with feats of grace and agility;
who will romp with children and work hard to con-
tribute his share to the general harmony.

Hair on the Back of the Hand

A hand that is hairy on the back betokens inconstancy, while a quite hairless and smooth hand denotes folly and presumption. A slight hairiness gives
prudence and a love of luxury to a man; but a hairy
hand on a woman always denotes cruelty.

Hair upon the thumb denotes ingenuity; on the third
and lower phalanges of the fingers only, it betrays
affection, and on all the phalanges a quick temper and
choleric disposition. Complete absence of hair upon the
hands betokens effeminacy and cowardice.

Color of the Hands

If the hands are continually white, never changing
color (or only very slightly) under the influences of
heat and cold, they denote egotism, selfishness and a

want of sympathy with the joys and sorrows of others.

Redness of the skin denotes sanguinity and hopefulness of temperament, yellowness denotes biliousness of disposition, blackness, melancholy, and pallor, a phlegmatic spirit. Darkness of tint is always preferable to paleness, which betrays effeminacy, the best color being a decided and wholesome rosiness which betokens a bright and just disposition.

CHAPTER VII

The study of the mounts forms the connecting link between Cheirognomy, or the general study of the hand, and Cheiromancy, or the study of the lines on the palm. Some palmists class them under one division, others under the other.

There are seven mounts, which are in reality slightly raised portions of the palm. They are indicated as follows:

Mount of *Jupiter*, at base of index finger.
Mount of *Saturn*, at base of middle finger.
Mount of *Apollo*, at base of ring finger.
Mount of *Mercury*, at base of little finger.
Mount of *Venus*, at base of the thumb.
Mount of the *Moon*, on side of hand opposite thumb.
Mount of *Mars*, between Mount of *Mercury* and that of the *Moon*.
Second Mount of *Mars*, influenced by *Jupiter*, under thumb, below *Venus*.

On a firm hand you will not see any marked rise when a mount is really very well developed. On the contrary, if it is wanting or badly developed, a hollow will be found. On a soft hand the mounts will be more prominent but will have no more significance than the lesser development on a hard hand. Thus it is manifest from the start that the type of hand must be taken into consideration in judging either mounts or lines. A hand may be callous from hard work and still the mounts will be unaffected.

The mounts will sometimes be found directly at the base of the fingers with which they are connected; but again they may lean much toward some other mount. A mount is said to be "good" when it is evenly developed, well-placed and firm when gently pressed. Then the quality belonging to it has been cultivated. It is said to be "unfavorable" when it encroaches that is, is overdeveloped and usurps another's position—is soft or absent. Then the qualities indicated are either in excess, or unused or wanting.

If the upper mounts are higher in proportion to the lower, it signifies predominance of the intellectual over the animal nature (just as in the case of long fingers, which will usually be found in connection with well-developed upper mounts). Should the lower mounts, or those on the wrist side of the palm, be in excess, then passion rules the life.

If all the mounts are flat it indicates practically an unemotional character, but they must be judged by gently pressing the sides of the hand together.

The mount which is highest in the hand will give the keynote to the character of the subject, and will be the first thing sought for. When the characteristics are thus pronounced by the development of a particular mount, the lesser development of another mount will indicate that the characteristics of the lesser will influence those of the greater, modifying, and in a manner perfecting those of the reigning development.

If a subject has no particularly prominent mount in his hand, that is, all mounts are equal, you will find a

singular regularity of mind and harmony of existence
to be his lot.

A mount may, instead of being high, be broad and
full, or it may be covered with little lines. These conditions of the mount give it the same effect as if it
were highly developed and it must be remarked that
if a mount is much covered by lines it will betray an
excess and overabundance of the qualities of the
mount. Excess of a mount does not give force, but
fever to its quality, producing monomanias, especially
if the thumb and the line of the head are weak.

One line upon a mount just emphasizes it enough to
be a fortunate sign; two lines show uncertainty in the
operation of the qualities especially if they are crossed;
and three, except in some rare cases, give misfortune
arising from the qualities of the mount, unless they be
even, straight and parallel. But it must be noted that in
hands of the long, thin, narrow type many lines may
be found without having the results here indicated,
while on a broad, hard, thick hand one line may have
the same effect as two on an average hand.

Lines placed crosswise upon a mount always denote
obstacles, and seriously interfere with the goodness of
other main lines which end upon the mount, as in the
cases of the mounts and lines of *Saturn* or of *Apollo*,
unless the ascending line is deeper than the cross line
in which case the evil indications of the cross line will
be destroyed.

In judging a mount always consider the lines upon
it, as well as its development. The one may counter-
balance the other.

Finally, the influence of the mount which is principally developed may be either good or bad. This may
be arrived at by inspecting the formation of the tips of
the fingers, the consistency of the hand and the development of the thumb. Thus, pointed fingers reveal an

intuition, a lofty idealism of the quality. Square fingers will look at the reasonable aspects of character and spatulate will cultivate the material qualities of the mount—for example, *Jupiter* developed will indicate with pointed fingers, religion; with square fingers, pride; with spatulate fingers, tyranny. *Apollo* developed will indicate with pointed fingers, love of glory; with square fingers realism in art; and with spatulate fingers love of wealth and luxury. And so on with the other mounts.

The Mount of Jupiter

The predominance of this mount in a hand denotes a genuine and reverential feeling of religion, a worthy and high ambition, honor, gaiety and a love of nature. It also indicates a love of display, of ceremony and of pomp, and is, consequently, generally developed in the hands of public entertainers of any sort.

An excessive development of the mount will give arrogance, tyranny, ostentation and with pointed fingers, superstition.

If the mount is absent (that is, replaced by a cavity), the subject is prone to idleness and egotism, irreligious feelings, want of dignity and a license which degenerates into vulgarity.

The development of this mount gives to the square hand a great love of regularity and established authority. To long, smooth fingers it imparts a love of luxury, especially if the fingers are large at the third phalanx. This mount ought always to be accompanied by a smooth, elastic, firm hand, not too hard, with a well-developed first phalanx of the thumb (will).

If to the good indications of this mount a favorably developed finger or Mount of *Saturn* is added, the success in life and good fortune of the subject is certain, *Saturn* denoting fatality, whether for good or evil.

A single line upon the mount denotes success. Many confused lines betray a constant, unsuccessful struggle for greatness, and if these lines are crossed they denote unchastity, no matter the sex of the subject.

A cross upon the mount denotes a happy marriage, and if a star is found there as well as the cross it indicates a brilliant and advantageous alliance.

A spot upon the mount indicates a fall from position and loss of honor or credit.

A long thumb and development of the first joint in the fingers will give to this mount free thought and irreverence in religion. If besides these we find pointed fingers and what is called the "Croix Mystique," you will find ecstasy in religious matters, tending even to fanaticism.

If the mount be displaced and leans toward *Saturn*, it gives a serious tone and demeanor and a desire for science, theology or classical scholarship.

Combined with a good development of the Mount of *Apollo* it indicates good fortune and wealth; with Mount of *Mercury*, love of exact science and philosophy. Such subjects (*Mercury* and *Jupiter*) make the most successful doctors. To a bad hand this combination gives egotism, fanaticism, charlatanry and immorality. Combined with *Mars* it gives audacity and the talent of strategy, and makes the subject self-confident and fond of celebrity, verging in a bad hand into insolence, dissipation and inconstancy. Combined with a good Mount of the *Moon* it makes the subject honorable, placid, and just. With a good Mount of *Venus* it gives the social, gay, sincere, generous friend; but with a bad hand this may become effeminacy, caprice and love of debauch.

Mount of Saturn

This mount is never very high. If it is at all prominent it denotes a character in which prudence and
natural caution are combined with a fatality for good
or evil. Such subjects are always sensitive and particular about little things, even when the fingers are
short. The mount also denotes a tendency to occult
science. Such subjects are inclined to be morbid and
melancholy. They are timid, and love solitude and a
quiet life in which there is neither great good fortune
nor great ill fortune. They like serious music better
than gay melody, and take naturally to pursuits of agriculture, horticulture or mineralogy, having a natural
penchant for anything connected with the earth.

Excessive development gives taciturnity, sadness, remorse and asceticism. They also may have an intense
fear and horror of death, and a morbid tendency toward and curiosity concerning suicide. Other features
of the hand may modify this, especially a well developed Mount of *Venus*.

The typical Saturnian hand has long, bony fingers.
A bad Saturnian hand gives rough skin and thick wrist.

If the mount is absent a depressed, unfortunate,
vegetable form of existence is indicated.

A single line on the mount indicates good fortune
and success; a succession of little lines placed ladder-
wise across the mount and extending over to the
Mount of *Jupiter* indicates an easy and steady pro-
gression to high honor. Many confused small lines
indicate ill luck.

A spot on the mount indicates an evil fatality, the
cause of which must be sought for on the lines of
Head or Fate.

If a branch (not the end) rises from the Heart Line
on to the Mount of *Saturn*, it denotes worry and

anxiety; but if it is clean and single it will denote wealth as a result of the anxiety.

No bad result is to be expected if the mount leans toward *Jupiter;* but a leaning toward *Apollo* betokens a fatality which must be striven against.

A cross on *Saturn* indicates sterility.

United with a good Mount of *Jupiter,* a well developed *Saturn* will give gentleness, patience and respect (in a good hand), or hysteria and want of taste in a bad hand. Combined with a well developed *Mercury,* it gives love of antiquarian research, love of science as a hobby, talent for medicine, and for classifying subjects. The combination usually results in happiness. In a bad hand the combination would indicate perfidy, perjury, revenge, theft, want of filial affection and charlatanry.

With a strong development of *Mars,* a strong Mount of *Saturn* indicates aggressiveness, bitterness of humor, a false superiority, insolence, immodesty and cynicism. Combined with a good Mount of *Venus* it gives piety, charity, self-control, with a tendency to jealousy and love of display. With a bad hand this combination betrays curiosity and frivolity and with *Saturn* predominating, even pride, envy and debauchery. With a well developed Mount of the *Moon,* Saturn gives a love of and talent for the occult; and, curiously enough, the subjects are usually frightfully ugly.

The Mount of Apollo

A hand in which this mount is developed is essentially that of a subject whose prevailing tastes and instincts are artistic. It always gives to its possessor a greater or less degree of success, glory, celebrity and brilliance of fortune, denoting genius, intelligence, tolerance and wealth; the characteristics of the type being self-confidence, beauty, grace and tolerance of all things, since all things are looked on merely as objects of art.

Such subjects are often great inventors. Their chief failings are a quick (though not lasting) temper, and a certain incapacity for close friendships, though they are generally benevolent and generous. Proud and eloquent on matters of art, they love everything which is brilliant, such as jewelry and the more ornamental forms of worship. They make stern and unrelenting judges, and their love is more affectionate than sensual.

These Apollonian subjects love to shine before the world and not to be cynosures of a small circle, though they hate the idea of ostentation or undeserved glory. In marriage they are often unlucky for their ideal is too high.

The normal development of a hand bearing this type shows smooth fingers with the tips mixed or slightly squared, the palm of an equal length with the fingers, a well-marked phalanx of logic, and either one very deep line or three strong lines upon the mount.

If this mount is developed to excess it denotes a love of wealth and extravagance, luxury, fatuity, envy and curiosity, a quick, unreasoning temper and a strong tendency to sophistry. Such subjects are boastful, vain, and think of themselves as highly superior to other men. In many cases they are superior, for among them will be found poets, painters and musicians, but their talents are too obtrusive to be attractive. This excess is accompanied, usually, by twisted fingers, a grille on the mount, or a long phalanx of will and a short phalanx of logic.

If the mount is absent in both hands it indicates a dull, unenlightened life, entirely without any appreciation of art or beauty.

A single line upon the mount indicates fortune and

glory, two lines indicate considerable talent, but
probability of failure and confused lines a tendency
to lean toward the scientific aspects of art.

If the mount is developed, but with no line upon it,
it shows a love of the beautiful, but not necessarily
any talent for producing works of art.

A spot indicates a grave danger of loss of reputa-
tion or caste.

When *Apollo* and *Mercury* are both well developed
we find a character in which justice, firmness, per-
spicacity, love of scientific research combined with
clearness of diction and eloquence are salient features.
Combined with a good Mount of the Moon, it gives
imagination and light-heartedness; with *Venus*, amiability and a desire to please.

Mount of Mercury

A well developed Mount of Mercury partly indicated by the fact that the fingers are set across the hand
in a straight line, the little finger no lower than the
rest, indicates eloquence, spirit, a capacity for commerce, speculation, industry and invention, agility and
promptitude in thought and action.

As to eloquence, the type of fingertips will indicate
its character. With a well-developed Mount of Mercury and pointed fingers, we get brilliant oratory; with
square fingers, clearness and reason in expounding;
with spatulate fingers, force and vehemence in argument and dogma; with long fingers, details and long-
windedness; with short fingers, brevity and concise-
ness.

A good Mount of Mercury makes good athletes,
spontaneous in ability, sharp in practice and with a
great capacity for serious study. There may be envy,
though usually combined with amiability.

These subjects are great matchmakers, frequently marry very young, choosing equally young persons as helpmates.

The normal hand which accompanies this is as follows: Long, smooth fingers, hard, slightly spatulated (athletics), or very soft with mixed tips (thought); the finger of *Mercury* long and sometimes pointed; the high mount cut by a deep line, and the philosophic joint developed.

If developed to excess *Mercury* makes thieves and cunning, treacherous and ignorant persons. These hands usually have long, twisted fingers, more or less turned back, soft hands and confused markings on the mount with long phalanx of will.

A single line on the mount indicates modesty and moderation, and often a stroke of good fortune. A crossed line extending upon the Mount of Apollo betrays the charlatan. Many mixed lines upon the mount indicate astuteness and aptitude for science. If the lines take the form of little flecks and dashes, it is a sure indication of a babbling, chattering disposition.

Lines on the percussion, or side of the hand, indicate liasons or serious affairs of the heart if horizontal; each line denoting a separate affair, a single deep line denoting one strong and lasting affection. Islands on these lines indicate unchastity or marriage to relatives, and an island on the line of *Saturn* or Fate indicates unfaithfulness to husband or wife.

A grille on the Mount of Mercury indicates violent death.

If there is a long line of *Apollo,* the commercial instincts given by *Mercury* will take the form of speculation. If the mount leans toward *Apollo* it indicates science and eloquence; if toward the percussion, commerce and industry. If a line connects it with the Mount of Venus, happiness and good fortune are indicated. Combined with a good Mount of Venus we have wit, humor, gaiety, love of beauty, often piety and easy sympathetic eloquence. In a bad hand this gives meddlesomeness, inconstancy and want of perseverance. A favorable combination with *Saturn* is always good; if with *Mercury* indicates business success, *Saturn* directs it toward land and building investments. The Mount of Mercury is, however, not often combined with the other mounts.

Mount of Mars

The Mount of Mars is not an easy subject to discuss. It consists of three separate divisions; first, the mount proper on the percussion of the hand between the Head and Heart lines, or between *Mercury* and the *Moon;* the center of the palm of the hand enclosed by the triangle formed by the lines of Heart, Health and Life, and known as the Plain of Mars; and the second Mount of Mars, situated within the Life Line under the Mount of Venus toward *Jupiter*. It will therefore be seen that *Mars* rules a belt across the middle of the hand from under the thumb to the percussion. The percussion side of *Mars* indicates resistance, endurance and stubborn courage. As the belt moves toward the thumb it indicates aggression, activity, pluck, fighting qualities, first in relation to the usual affairs of life, in business, and then in the social world and in the seeking of honors and positions. The development between *Jupiter* and *Venus* the present writer believes indicates mental activity and energy. It must be admitted, however, that students of cheirology differ widely on this subject, which indicates lack of observation upon the matter.

The following remarks apply to the Mount of Mars

on the percussion—the chief division of the *Mars* influence.

Well developed and not covered by lines or rays it gives calmness and resignation which to a considerable extent will overcome the bad effects of a small thumb. Such a person will keep his temper, will be magnanimous, generous, loud of voice and hot blooded, his passions carrying him even to sensuality unless counteracted by a strong phalanx of logic.

Mars has a natural attraction toward *Venus*. Fighting men are also particularly given to love and cut a large figure in the eyes of women, since admiration is mutual.

The hands to which these martial mounts belong are usually hard, the fingers large, especially at the third phalanx, the will long and the logic small, the hollow of the hand rayed and lined. If the mount spreads into the palm, or is covered by a mass of lines, it indicates fury, injustice of mind, insolence, violence, cruelty, insult and defiance of manner. A network of lines on the Plain of Mars indicates obstacles in the way of real good fortune due to overaggressiveness.

Absence of the mount denotes cowardice and weakness of character.

Combined with a well-developed Mount of the Moon *Mars* indicates a love of navigation, or on a bad hand folly. Combined with *Venus* it indicates love of music, dancing and jealousy in love.

The Plain of Mars

The Plain of Mars is the space lying in the center of the hand and bounded by the lines of Heart, Life and Health. It shows the aggressiveness of the subject. If very high and hard great combativeness is shown. If hollow, submission either to circumstances or health. This hollow is observed by Cheiro to incline more to one line than to another and he gives the following readings:

A hollow under the Line of Life, domestic troubles.

Under the Line of Fate, disappointment in business.

Under the line of Apollo, failure in art and position.

A failure in the top of the Quadrangle under the Heart Line shows disappointment in "the dearest affections."

Care must be taken to distinguish between a really hollow palm and a palm that appears so by reason of the height of the mounts surrounding it.

Mount of the Moon

The attributes of this mount (the side of the palm extending from the wrist half way to the base of the little finger) when found predominant in a hand are imagination, melancholy, chastity, poetry of soul and a love of mystery, solitude, and silence with a tendency to reverie and imagination. It is also connected with harmony in music, as *Venus* gives melody.

Such subjects are capricious, changeable and inclined to be idle. They may have prophetic dreams and presentiments; they are fond of travel; are mystics in religion and given to romance in art and literature. They lack self-confidence and powers of conversation; eloquence is usually wanting. They are much given to capricious marriages.

These hands are usually small and soft, with short, smooth and pointed fingers and a short phalanx of logic. To be at its best the mount should be most developed toward the wrist as development toward Mars at the center of the palm indicates ill health.

The mount developed with a hard hand often denotes a dangerous activity of the imagination; with spatulate fingers it makes schemers. An excessive development produces irritability, discontent, sadness, superstition, fanaticism and error, with liability to headaches and morbidity. If the mount is absent it denotes want of all imagination. Many lines upon the mount indicate visions and prophetic dreams; this is also the result of a line from the Mount of Mercury to the Mount of the Moon.

Lines on the percussion extending horizontally indicate voyages, and a star upon one of these a dangerous ending to a voyage. A star on the mount connected by a line with the Line of Life indicates hysteria or incipient insanity. The mount much crossed indicates much worry.

An equal development of the *Moon* and *Mercury* denotes subtlety and intuition in the deeper sciences, bringing (with other favorable signs) success and celebrity. Combined with a good Mount of Venus it gives curiosity and a romantic, fantastic view of affairs of the heart. In a bad hand it gives caprice, eccentricity and unnatural instincts.

THE MOUNTS

MOUNT OF JUPITER

Good.	*Excess.*
Pride and self-respect.	Conceit.

Wanting.
Lack of self-respect.

MOUNT OF SATURN

Love of solitude and agriculture.	Morbidness.

Frivolity.

MOUNT OF APOLLO

Mercy and talent.   Mercy without justice,
                                    gambling.
                    Cruelty, dullness.

MOUNT OF MERCURY

Buoyancy, cheerfulness,   Chattering, indifference
    talkativeness.   to feelings of others.
                    No sense of humor.

MOUNT OF MARS

Power of endurance.   Stolidity.
                    Cowardice.

MOUNT OF THE MOON

Imagination and   Eccentricity.
    originality.

                    No imagination.

MOUNT OF VENUS

Affection.   Sensuality.
                    Coldness.

Mount of Venus

The Mount of Venus includes the large muscle at
the base of the thumb and covers more space than any
other mount. Nearly all hands have some prominence
here. If the hand is quite flat the mount may be said
to be wanting; when large it forms a decided prominence over nearly the whole space included within the
Line of Life.

Its attributes are possession of, and admiration for,
beauty, grace, melody in music, dancing, gallantry,
tenderness and benevolence with a constant desire to
please and to be appreciated. It is found to be well

developed in all singers, as it may be called preeminently the Mount of Melody. It indicates the peculiarly feminine forms of beauty, the masculine being indicated by *Jupiter*.

When well developed, this mount makes lovers of pleasure, applause, poetry and music. It makes men effeminate to some extent but it softens the malignities of other mounts which are bad.

The type of hand in which this mount is usually found well developed is fat, dimpled, with smooth rather short fingers and short thumb. The bad type is accompanied by an extremely soft hand, pointed fingers and many crossbar lines on the mount. An excess of the mount will indicate license, vanity, flirtation and levity. The absence of the mount indicates coldness and dullness in matters of art, making the other passions dry and selfish. If completely devoid of lines (more lines are to be found on this mount than on any other) it indicates coldness and in many cases short life. A great number of lines indicate the heat of passion and warmth of temperament. Two or three deep lines are said to indicate ingratitude. A wornout libertine usually has this mount flat but much rayed and the Girdle of Venus clearly traced.

A line from the middle of the mount to the base of the hand rising into the middle of the mount is a sign of good luck.

Islands on lines of the mount indicate lost opportunities for marriages. Lines from the phalanx of logic on to the mount are said to indicate marriages. Little moons on the mount are said to indicate adultery.

Jupiter is called the "social mount," and gives kindness to animals. *Mars* indicates reserve.

Lines on the Mounts

Jupiter. Lines crossing the mount from *Venus* to *Saturn*, family misfortunes.

Lines crossing branches of the Heart Line on the mount, misfortune in love. Lines rising from the Life Line toward *Jupiter* indicate changes for the better.

A line from the Fate Line or Line of Fortune turning toward *Jupiter* indicates change for the better in social position or money.

A triangle on the mount shows ambitious diplomacy.

Saturn. Many crossed lines forming a star, ill health and trouble at close of life.

One deep line forming the end of the Fate Line indicates a peaceful and monotonous ending.

A line across the Fate Line on the mount shows unavoidable misfortune.

A triangle is said to show a taste for black magic.

Apollo. One deep line running as the finger runs shows one career; two lines, various interests.

A forked line shows conflicting careers.

A line across the mount from base of *Saturn*, unavoidable money loss.

A line rising from *Venus* and crossing the *Apollo* Line on the mount shows loss of money from some member of the family late in life.

A triangle is said to show science in art.

Mercury. A deeply marked line running as does the finger shows scientific tastes.

Several lines, medical science; in the hand of a woman they show the nurse.

A line across the mount toward *Apollo* would show loss through theft.

A triangle, craft in politics.

Mars (percussion). Lines across the percussion show enemies, which may be judged by the length and depth. Small cross lines are said to show scandal. If the lines cross the Hepatica, *Apollo*, or Fate lines, they show interference which affects health, money or career. If the lines extend to *Venus* it is relatives who are malignant.

Mars (under thumb). A deep groove across the mount toward the Life Line indicates dread of physical pain, though when the other Mount of Mars is high pain is borne well.

Lines from base of thumb across toward *Jupiter* show family influence.

Lines crossing the mount toward the Fate Line show worries from members of the family. If they touch the Head Line, mental troubles; if the Heart Line, deep sorrow.

Luna. Lines rising upward from the Rascettes across *Luna* toward *Mars* show long voyages.

Lines crossing transversely, various travels. If deeply marked, pleasant; crossed, broken or islanded generally unpleasant; with squares, dangers escaped.

Innumerable lines crossing Luna show nervous complaints and neuralgia.

A triangle is said to show mysticism.

A straight line from the percussion to *Venus* shows intemperance; ending with a dot, delirium tremens.

Venus. Lines crossing from the base of the thumb to the Life Line show the people with whom you have principally had to deal. A triangle is said to show calculation in love.

CHAPTER VIII

Summary of Characteristics. (An Alphabetically Arranged Table of Qualities and Their Signs in the Hand).

The following summary of qualities or characteristics and their signs will be found of great utility in answering questions easily and quickly:

Acquisitiveness: Fingers curved inward and no stretch between first finger and thumb.

Adaptability: A flexible thumb, especially at first joint; flexible palm and fingers.

Anger: Red nails (square bases show revenge), low mounts of Mars (they give control when developed).

Art: For painting, long fingers for detail, short for effects; large hands; Mount of the Moon well developed for imagination and originality; *Mercury* high for the imitative quality; first phalanx of *Apollo* long and wide for form and color; Mount of Apollo high for animal painting. For sculpture, rather small hands, long fingers (knots no objection), the first phalanx of all the fingers long for deftness in detail, *Apollo* finger dominant for distinction in form, and mounts of Luna and Mercury high for originality and imitativeness. For the drama, long fingers, *Mercury* dominant; turned back thumb; good mounts of Mercury and Luna; *Saturn* mount and finger dominant for tragedy; percussion *(Mars* and *Mercury)* developed for comedy. (These combinations would give the ideal artist.)

Ambition: Long, strong and straight finger of *Jupiter;* high mount, and cross on second phalanx for social ambition; first phalanx of *Apollo* finger wide and long in addition gives artistic ambition, a long and dominant *Mercury* finger; good thumb, the ambition to business; good first phalanx of *Mercury* turns the ambition to diplomacy.

Analysis: Long, knotted fingers for investigation; short nails for criticism; well developed second phalanx of thumb for logic.

Benevolence: Mount of *Venus* for emotion; *Luna* for

sympathy; thumb for constancy; stretch between first finger and thumb for generosity.

Bohemianism: Long, widely separated fingers, flexible palm, sloping Head Line, short turned back thumb and well developed *Luna.*

Calculation: Long, knotted fingers; long finger of *Mercury* (squared).

Caprice: Short first phalanx of thumb, short fingers, soft hand.

Concentration: Long fingers, long and strong thumb.

Conventionality: Straight, stiff fingers set close together, stiff palm, straight thumb.

Construction: Long first phalanges of all fingers spatulated and mounts of *Mercury* and *Moon.*

Courage: Both mounts of *Mars* high and hard, Plain of *Mars* high, *Saturn* low, and *Luna* not very high. This gives extreme courage of an almost brutal type. A good Mount of *Mars* on the percussion alone will give passive courage.

Courtesy: Medium palm and fingers flexible, Plain of *Mars* not too high, and mounts of *Jupiter, Luna* and *Mercury* well developed.

Craft: Long finger of *Mercury* (dominant), and strong thumb.

Deceit: Long finger of *Mercury,* and high Mount of *Luna.* Liars with poor memory and little imagination from low *Luna* are successful in their deceit.

Devotion: For religious devotion subject should have long, pointed finger of *Jupiter,* pointed thumb, *Luna* developed toward wrist, and soft palm, high mounts of *Saturn* and *Venus.*

Eccentricity: Mount of *Luna* highly developed, sometimes with excrescences.

Egotism: Thick, white, firm palm, high Mount of *Jupiter,* low *Luna* and *Mercury.*

Energy: Hard, firm palm, well developed Plain of Mars.

Enmity: Lines on *Mars* denote enemies; short nails square at base; high mounts on *Saturn* and *Luna.*

Economy: Stiff thumb, long knotted fingers.

Eloquence: Long fingers of *Mercury* and *Jupiter* and high mounts of *Luna* and *Mercury.*

Fatalism: Heavy finger and Mount of *Saturn*, soft, hollow palm and thumb turned outward.

Firmness: Long, equally balanced thumb, knotted fingers that are fairly long.

Foolishness: Weak first phalanx of thumb, soft hand.

Gratitude: Good thumb, high mounts of *Venus* and *Luna.*

Heroism: High mounts of *Mars, Luna* and *Venus.*

Honesty: Straight finger of *Jupiter* and good thumb.

Idiocy: Twisted fingers, turned in thumb and a hand altogether badly developed.

Idleness: Soft, fat palm with no knuckles visible.

Impulse: Short fingers, small thumb.

Justice: Long, straight finger of *Jupiter*, long and strong thumb.

Love: Platonic love is given by a strong thumb and small lines running parallel. Friendship is given by high mounts of *Luna* and *Venus.* Passionate love is indicated by high mounts of *Luna* and *Venus* and many encroaching influence lines, with a weak thumb (allowing the love to rule the life).

Madness: Head Line broken and drooping to Luna; high mounts of *Saturn* and *Luna.* If *Mercury* is absent and there are stars on *Mars*, the madness will be homicidal.

Melancholy: Long, heavy finger and Mount of *Saturn*, no Mount of *Mercury* and a development of *Luna* toward the wrist (generally long, knotted fingers).

Method: Both knots, long fingers and thumb.

Narrow-mindedness: Quadrangle very narrow, fingers and thumb conventional.

Occultism: Long, smooth fingers, *Luna* developed toward wrist, Line of Intuition present, and the *croix mystique* in quadrangle.

Order: Long, knotted fingers; straight Head Line.

Perception: The first phalanx of all the fingers cushioned and Mount of *Luna* developed.

Practicability: Hard hand, medium palm and fingers, good thumb.

Pride: Long finger of *Jupiter,* especially third phalanx, long and high Mount of *Jupiter.* If Mount of *Jupiter* leans toward Venus we have family pride.

Prudence: Evenly developed and strong thumb, finger of *Saturn* well but not too well developed.

Reason: Long second phalanx of thumb, medium palm and fingers.

Religion: Straight finger of *Jupiter* pointed, long first phalanx of *Mercury* finger giving eloquence, straight and well developed thumb. (This analysis applies to clergymen.)

Reverence: Long, smooth finger of *Jupiter.*

Sociability: Developed Mount of *Jupiter,* Mount of *Mercury* and medium palm and fingers.

Tact: Long, pointed first phalanx of *Mercury.*

Timidity: Depression at base of third phalanx, depression of *Mars* on percussion, hollow palm.

Vanity: High Mount of *Jupiter* sloping toward the base of the finger.

Wit: Mount of *Mercury* and finger well developed, first phalanx long for repartee; *Mars* under *Mercury* well developed.

YOUR FORTUNE REVEALED BY YOUR DREAMS

With The Aid of a Regular Deck of
Playing Cards and the Planetary
Timetable.

DIRECTIONS

To learn the meaning of any dream on any day, use
the planetary timetable to find the planet that rules the
day following your dream. For example: If you remember a dream on the morning of Monday, the 6th of the
month, refer to the planetary timetable and you will
find that the planet Saturn rules Monday, the 6th.

Take a regular deck of playing cards, shuffle them
three times, cut the cards with your left hand, then
select a card at random from the deck (Cards from
ace to ten retain their regular numbers, Jacks are
counted as number eleven, Queens as number twelve
and Kings as number thirteen.)

If the card you select is Number five, turn to the
paragraph on Saturn's reply. Read the prediction for
number Five, which says "a Fortunate dream, but not
very important."

Many important messages have been obtained by
using this ancient gypsy method of divining omens
from dreams.

YOUR GUIDING CHART

	DAY OF THE WEEK						
DAY of the MONTH	SUNDAY	MONDAY	TUESDAY	WEDNESDAY	THURSDAY	FRIDAY	SATURDAY
1-	SATURN	SATURN	JUPITER	MARS	VENUS	MERCURY	MOON
2-	SUN	MERCURY	VENUS	MARS	JUPITER	SATURN	VENUS
3-	JUPITER	VENUS	MARS	MERCURY	MOON	SUN	MERCURY
4-	VENUS	MARS	JUPITER	SATURN	SATURN	JUPITER	MARS
5-	JUPITER	MERCURY	MOON	SUN	MERCURY	VENUS	MARS
6-	VENUS	SATURN	SATURN	JUPITER	MARS	VENUS	MERCURY
7-	MOON	SUN	MERCURY	VENUS	MARS	JUPITER	SATURN
8-	SATURN	JUPITER	MERCURY	VENUS	MERCURY	MOON	SUN
9-	MERCURY	VENUS	MARS	JUPITER	SATURN	SATURN	JUPITER
10-	MARS	VENUS	MERCURY	MOON	SUN	MERCURY	VENUS
11-	MERCURY	JUPITER	SATURN	SATURN	JUPITER	MARS	VENUS
12-	SATURN	MOON	SUN	MERCURY	VENUS	MARS	JUPITER
13-	SATURN	SATURN	JUPITER	MARS	VENUS	MERCURY	MOON
14-	SUN	MERCURY	VENUS	MARS	JUPITER	SATURN	SATURN
15-	JUPITER	MARS	VENUS	MERCURY	MOON	SUN	MERCURY
16-	VENUS	MARS	JUPITER	SATURN	SATURN	JUPITER	MARS
17-	JUPITER	MERCURY	MOON	SUN	MERCURY	VENUS	MARS
18-	SATURN	SATURN	SATURN	JUPITER	MARS	VENUS	MERCURY
19-	MOON	SUN	MERCURY	VENUS	MARS	JUPITER	SATURN
20-	SATURN	JUPITER	MARS	VENUS	MERCURY	MOON	SUN
21-	MERCURY	VENUS	MERCURY	JUPITER	SATURN	SATURN	JUPITER
22-	MARS	VENUS	SATURN	SATURN	SUN	MERCURY	VENUS
23-	MARS	JUPITER	SUN	MERCURY	JUPITER	MARS	VENUS
24-	MERCURY	MOON	JUPITER	MARS	VENUS	MARS	JUPITER
25-	SUN	SATURN	VENUS	MERCURY	JUPITER	MERCURY	MOON
26-	JUPITER	MERCURY	VENUS	MARS	MOON	SATURN	SATURN
27-	VENUS	MARS	JUPITER	MERCURY	SATURN	SUN	MERCURY
28-	VENUS	MARS	MOON	SUN	MERCURY	JUPITER	MARS
29-	JUPITER	MERCURY	SATURN	JUPITER	MARS	VENUS	MARS
30-	JUPITER	SATURN	MERCURY	SATURN	MARS	VENUS	MERCURY
31-	MOON	SUN			JUPITER	MARS	VENUS

THE SUN'S REPLY

1. You misjudge your friend.
2. Do not give way to discontentment.
3. One of the opposite sex is deceiving you.
4. A dream that foretells some gaiety.
5. You are deceiving yourself.
6. Love is waiting. Your own folly is a bar.
7. Be careful over documents.
8. Good luck awaits.
9. Do not make any change without careful thought.
10. A dream of no importance.
11. Business prosperity.
12. Beware of impatience.
13. You have a friend whose worth you do not value rightly.

THE MOON'S REPLY

1. It is a dream of memory.
2. You have won the love of many.
3. Why should you hesitate in your choice?
4. Someone loves you in silence.
5. An absent friend is thinking of you.
6. Make sure the one you love is worthy.
7. Be strong to fight temptation.
8. Love will bring happiness if you are true.
9. Do not lose heart.
10. Happiness is near. Do not look far away.
11. Beware of a jealous rival.
12. It is a very good dream. Wait and see.
13. An unexpected gift.

MERCURY'S REPLY

1. Prosperity and new business.

2. A faithless friend.
3. The journey will lead to good fortune.
4. The old love is true.
5. A change for the better.
6. Do not tell this dream. Wait.
7. Travel is favorable.
8. Happiness is ahead.
9. A disappointment is approaching.
10. The money will be paid.
11. Be true to your friend.
12. Yes, that journey will lead to good fortune.
13. News from a sailor or someone overseas.

VENUS' REPLY

1. You are trusting those who are false.
2. Your wish will be granted.
3. Quarrels.
4. The letter you long for.
5. A dream with no meaning.
6. Much anxiety and many changes.
7. Unexpected visitors.
8. Value the love you have won.
9. A surprise.
10. Those money troubles will pass.
11. Slanderous tongues are speaking.
12. Illness is indicated, not necessarily your own.
13. A new friend.

MARS' REPLY

1. Your dream is fortunate.
2. Wait and see.
3. A disappointment that ought not to be.
4. Do not continue the quarrel.
5. News is on its way.

6.   It is foolish to worry without cause.
7.   You will have what you deserve.
8.   The dream is only a sign of indigestion.
9.   No, your wish will not be granted.
10. Your friend is true.
11. Disappointment.
12. Good news is coming.
13. Keep on as you are doing.

JUPITER'S REPLY

1.   The best of good luck.
2.   A secret enemy.
3.   It is not important.
4.   You will hear of a wedding.
5.   An obstacle is in your way.
6.   Jealousy will kill love. Be careful.
7.   Do not make that change without grave thought. Doubtful.
8.   Good fortune is at hand.
9.   You give way to depression. The cloud has a silver lining.
10. Your wish will be granted.
11. Happiness lies ahead.
12. Illness is indicated. It may be a long way off.
13. That love is yours.

SATURN'S REPLY

1.   News of an engagement.
2.   Avoid quarrels.
3.   You will meet a dear friend.
4.   A removal.
5.   A fortunate dream, but not important.
6.   The letter will tell you what you want to know.
7.   Great caution is required.

8. Do not be hasty.
9. A warning of accident.
10. Happy love is yours if you are sensible.
11. One who is now a stranger will influence you.
12. No, what you expect will not happen.
13. Why not trust your friend?